A Pinch of Coriander

Available Now

A Pinch of Coriander:
Book One
Time Will Tell

A Pinch of Coriander:
Book Two
The Truth About Secrets

A Pinch of Coriander:
Book Three
Long Way Home

A Pinch of Coriander

Book One:
Time Will Tell

Loretta Gatto-White

© 2021 by Loretta Gatto-White
All rights reserved
First Edition 2021

Loretta Gatto-White, Publisher: https://gattowhitewrites.com

Cover designed by Kate Cowan

ISBN 978-1-7750341-0-0 (Paper Back edition)
ISBN 978-1-7750341-1-7 (eBook edition)

Print Edition

Chapter One

Winter

THE KNIGHTS OF SAN LORENZO

THE LOADING DOCKS' steel doors boomed closed, at Toronto's St. Lawrence Market, startling the pigeons huddled in the rafters. Wool-capped porters careered down the aisles with their now empty wagons, hurrying towards a hot breakfast. The vendors grumbled and fussed over their bounty's display. The cavernous space warmed-up as the massive boilers reached full throttle and the Saturday morning crush of parka-clad patrons expanded by the minute, their warm heavy breath, diffuse in the dank morning air.

'Grrrr' Nick's stomach rumbled audibly as a calf-skin glove cuffed his right shoulder, jiggling the steaming coffee raised to his thirsty lips.

"Hey, watch it, Javi!" Nick shouted at his friend.

"Whoa, Nick, you hungry or just swallowed a mad dog?"

"You're late, and yes I'm hungry, you idiot," Nick

answered, with a frown.

"Well, a 'top o'the mornin' to you too, you old misery," Javi retorted in a cheery 'stage Irish'.

"Piss-off Javi, I'm not old."

"That's enough fighting, boys," admonished Father Frank as he advanced towards his friends. "Now, it's down on your knees and give me five Hail Mary's each."

"Uh-oh!" exclaimed Paul, popping-up behind the huddled group. "I thought that posture was reserved for your altar boys."

"Shut-up, Paul," all three shot back together.

The four 'boomers' grew-up together in a Catholic choir school where they learned to intone eerily celestial sounds that soared to the heights of the gilded grandeur of St. Michael's Cathedral, Toronto. Nick, Javier, Frank, and Paul remained close friends since their choir school days. All but Frank had left the church behind.

The freckled, blue-eyed ringer for Robert Redford joined it, finally making his pious, widowed mother, Mrs. Kelley, content as he was her only child, and her last shot at salvation. Her husband, Frank senior, being killed in a motor vehicle accident while on duty as a newly minted Ontario Provincial Police officer, just four years after emigrating from England with their young son.

Nick, or Nero, as his parents christened their only son, was forty-nine, swarthy like most of his father's Calabrese clan, green-eyed, barrel-chested, and stockily built; in short, he looked more like a middle-weight boxer than a professor of Renaissance Art. A devoted epicurean, his passion for all things culinary, a blessing to his busy wife Lidia, perpetually hungry daughter Jesse, and live-in father-in-law, Aldo.

His closest friend of the group was Javier, his name pronounced in the South American manner as Havier, abbreviated to Havi by his friends. His family was of mysterious Argentine origins, rumored tied to the Peronist regime and that low friends in high places helped them flee the revolution with their fortune intact. The official line though, was that they were simply merchants seeking greener pastures in Canada.

Javier was tall, fair, and patrician in contrast to his easy-going, suave demeanor and enthusiasm for the sybaritic pleasures this mean world has to offer. Being President of Merchandise in his family's fine food, spice and wine import business, an occupation taking him all over the world, well-suited his restless spirit.

If Javi was the high-flyer of the group, then Paul was certainly the groundling, an earthy, wiry carpenter, owner of a high-end flooring company. A hard-working suburbanite father of three teenage girls, Paul called the three Hecates, the only part of his high-school brush with Shakespeare that rubbed-off; Macbeth's mixture of sex, murder and witchcraft created a potent potion for his adolescent imagination.

Now, their sweet vocal harmony, having soured over too much tobacco, vinho tinto and time, it is their love of food, the gathering, making, and sharing that forms their enduring bond. The spirited act of creation, whether of a chorale or a robust meal, takes *simpatico* to lovingly execute.

This was their monthly ritual, to gather at their hometown's oldest market, to pursue the best, indulging their senses in the repast it will become under Nick's direction and imbibing Javi's free-flowing libation, to sustain their spirits.

"Why is everyone so late? Two minutes more and I would've had my mitts around a hot 'three-b' without you," replied Nick, referring to their ritual back bacon on a bun for which the market was famous.

"No prizes for guessing which half of that 'sangwich' would have the most hog," taunted Paul, whose own stomach was suddenly feeling deprived.

The smell of the first bacon slices hitting the

sizzling grill beckoned them to their feast, "Well, c'mon guys, let's move it, before the lineup starts," urged Nick, as he turned toward the kiosk.

All their orders were alike and never varied, always a toasted Kaiser with lettuce, piled high with hot grilled back bacon topped with mustard, and black coffees all round. Toasting the Kaiser bun stopped it from absorbing too much of the warm bacon juices. The iceberg lettuce gave it a fresh crunch and the mustard, hotdog Heinz, never anything fancy like Dijon, formed the perfect complement of sweet, spice and vinegar to the salty bacon; heaven on a bun, so primal, unpretentious and satisfying.

Thus fortified, the men turned to their morning's quest, predicated on what Nick had devised for the menu. This could vary though, depending upon the quality of the ingredients needed and what else might be improvised with something fresh and interesting that Nick hadn't counted on seeing.

The highlight of today's menu consisted of a dish the friends had made many times before, Nick's own version of the classic Bolognese ragù on homemade pappardelle, which was the primo. The antipasti would be some finocchiona, a Tuscan fennel seed salami, then slices of smoked peppercorn pecorino, Spanish queen olives served in a warm marinade of lemon, rosemary and vermouth, and pickled sweet red cherry peppers stuffed with parsley, capers, and anchovies. Secondo was another favorite, baby eggplant ripieni; small eggplants blanched, scooped out, then stuffed with their sautéed pulp, onions, parmesan, and breadcrumbs, tops brushed with egg white and pan-fried upside down; a golden-crusted delicacy. An endive, walnut and gorgonzola salad would add a touch of bitter green.

It was often the case that they didn't get around to dessert, but Nick felt that muscat grapes and panna cotta, made with a fruity grappa that Javier discovered would be a nice dénouement. In fact, since Javi was supplying the wines, an Umbrian sagrantino, a new Ferrari spumante, and the subtle but key ingredient for the Bolognese sauce, a packet of sweet fresh coriander seeds, their morning's quest was simplified.

Their personal shopping was not confined to the list, as they usually purchased treats like farm fresh sweet butter, and specialty cheeses from small artisan producers. Then they would meander across the street to the North Market, where the local organic producers were who came in from the dwindling rural greenbelts of farming communities surrounding the sprawling monster that was the 'GTA' or Greater Toronto Area.

They purveyed excellent organic produce, meat,

poultry, game and fresh seasonal vegetables like cardoons, radicchio Treviso and Boston Red Jerusalem artichokes. And foraged gems like cicoria, wild asparagus, nettles, ramps, giant puffballs, and fragrant chanterelles. Laden with their culinary treasures they squeezed into Nick's Honda and headed for his Victorian semi in east Toronto just south of Danforth Avenue, or 'The Danny' as it denizens affectionately called it.

The Ponti family lived in the gentrified Playter Estates, on a leafy winding street in a neighborhood transitioning from its post-war Greek and Italian immigration to the arrival in the nineties of the Muslim nations, who built mosques and replaced mom and pop Italian groceries with halal meat markets, and souvlaki joints with take-out curry kitchens.

For the most part, the three main religious communities, Greek Orthodox, Roman Catholic and Muslim lived side-by-side peacefully and without incident, their children attending the same schools, playing in the same parks, and making mischief together in the same back alleys and parking lots.

MANNA AND CORIANDER

USUALLY GRACEFUL AND well-coordinated, Lidia Ponti cut an awkward figure as she tried with one hand to hold a slippery bag of dry cleaning and a bouquet of subway flowers, while the arm supporting her briefcase strained to reach the doorbell; the effort set her back on her heels, precariously balanced on the very narrow, top step of her front porch.

"Shit! How long have I been asking for new front steps? These bloody things are a hazard!"

Her husband opened the door, interrupting her diatribe. "Eh, Nick, how long? Twenty-two years, that's how long!" Lidia complained loudly.

"I thought I heard you bellowing out here. C'mon, give me your things, the guys are here; go have a glass of wine with them."

"Just need to nip upstairs first, be down in a minute."

Lidia sprang-up the long flight of stairs to their front bedroom, where she exchanged her thick loose turtleneck for a white Egyptian cotton shirt that draped and felt like satin, then put on a silver necklace whose large blue topaz pendant sat prettily at the top of her cleavage and reflected the color of her wide-open eyes. She spritzed a little cologne on her brush, ran it through her shoulder-length gold hi-lited hair, applied a touch of tinted gloss to the curve of her full lips, checked her 'Spanx-lines', wriggled comically while tugging the restrictive garment into place, then headed downstairs to join the men.

"Mmm, smells like heaven in here," Lidia said as she brushed past her husband arranging the flowers in a colorful majolica pitcher.

"You're pretty fragrant yourself or is that the flowers?" asked Nick.

"Me and the flowers."

Then turning towards her husband's friends, each busy at their station, Paul at the Wolf gas range sautéing a sofrito: the 'holy trinity' of finely chopped onions, celery and carrots, the base for the Bolognese sauce. Frank was at the antique harvest table assiduously kneading the dough for the pasta and Javi at the granite-top island, fastidious as always, carefully stuffing the cherry peppers. She made her rounds, greeting each with a kiss on the cheek and a charming smile, a welcome interruption as they were all a little smitten with Lidia.

Javi wiped his long, elegant fingers on the towel draped over his shoulder and poured his hostess some sparkling wine in a tall Riedel flute, "Try a bit of this Lidia, it's a new spumante I'm bringing in, nice minerality, crisp, but with a little surprise finish."

"Cin-cin!" She raised her glass and sipped thoughtfully. "Very nice, that hint of lychee softens the minerality, more complex than most brut Champagne."

Javi smiled approvingly at her critique. "Your palate, as your beauty Lidia, is unfailing."

"Just listen to 'Signor soave bolla' here – lock-up your wives and daughters," laughed Frank.

"And your sheep," enjoined Paul.

They were all laughing when Aldo appeared in the doorway.

"Hey, here's the man," declared Javi, placing a full flute at Aldo's undisputed perch at the head of the wooden table.

"What's this about sheep?" he asked in a voice still thick with sleep.

"Oh, nothing, we were just having a laugh on Javi," explained Nick as he pulled out his father-in-law's well-worn chair.

Once seated, Lidia kissed the top of his grey head. "Ciao dad, how's the cold? Did you have a good nap?"

"I dreamt of lizards, uch, I hate that dream. Same thing, they coming out of the drains and the crapper, slithering around, I hate them!" He shuddered and then turned his attention to the spumante. He sipped the cool, bubbly wine through puckered lips, tentatively, as if unsure of its potability. "Very nice," he declared.

Sparkling wines weren't something he usually cared for on account of their chilling effect on the stomach and the unwanted gas they created, but he hated to be ungracious to such a dear family friend. Setting the flute aside, a silent cue for his daughter to fetch him a glass of Chianti, he pursued the theme of his worrying dream. "Eh, professore! What's it mean, dreaming of lizards slithering everywhere, green lizards with eyes like flames?"

"Mean?" replied Nick. "It means you shouldn't watch the Nature Channel before a nap."

Aldo shrugged his shoulders and chuckled at his son-in-law's little joke, made to diffuse his father-in-law's anxiety about death, a subject which seemed to be on his mind lately.

"I hope you're in the mood for pasta, Nick's making his special Bolognese ragù," offered Lidia.

"Good, that ragù is very nice with a little pinch of coriander, not typical, but nice all the same." Then he put down his glass, and made for the sitting room, where every Saturday afternoon he liked to listen to the radio and read the paper, checking the winners from last night's race.

Aldo Campanile was fond of the ponies and even fonder of winning long-shots, a surprisingly lucrative habit he acquired during his forty-five years at The Jockey Club, first as a dishwasher, then a line cook, eventually becoming a sous-chef, his specialties being the classics, soused salmon, lobster thermidor and sole meuniere.

Growing-up in a family restaurant in the Italian Adriatic port of Pescara, he had acquired a knack with seafood which the exclusive membership of The Jockey Club's high-rolling patrons; sports' scions, star athletes, financiers, celebrities, and gangsters appreciated and especially asked for whenever they were in town or entertaining an important guest. The soused salmon required a twenty-four-hour pre-order, a request that he might be called upon to prepare off hours, depending upon the patron's status.

This devoted following helped to finally move him to the front of the house, being maître'd for the last ten years of his tenure, a position he had always coveted.

"That paesan, is where you wanna be," advised a friend who tended bar at The King Edward Hotel's piano lounge. "Great tips, and the inside track, buddy, know what I mean?"

Aldo did, keeping his ears open and his eyes

down. There were four important qualities in a good maître'd; listen, but never appear to be, anticipate but never presume, be attentive and not intrusive. Above all, be discreet, for not only did one in his position over-hear gossip, political intrigue and byzantine plots involving the sports' world, there was the matter of women. There were the wives, who were sometimes feted, but foremost were the reigning coterie of professional mistresses and the lesser occasional 'escorts', these ladies changed tables often, so to spare his patrons embarrassment or social scandal, the maître'd's job was to inform, guide and arrange the guests, who showed their appreciation generously.

He did the job well and it did well by him, providing decently for his wife and child, his late wife needing only to work part-time outside the home in a hospital laundry. They owned their house, took modest vacations, splurging on their twenty-fifth anniversary to take a deluxe Mediterranean cruise and send their only child to art college while managing to build a small retirement fund. A fund his wife, Filomena never lived long enough to enjoy, dying suddenly of an aneurism at fifty-seven.

That was twelve years ago. Aldo overcame the shock and grief, but never the love for his adored 'Filly', learning to cry alone, but never to laugh alone.

His major consolation, his talented and beautiful daughter Lidia, a newly appointed magazine editor, wife and mother, whose family he now lived with, in relative content.

Although Aldo was retired from his work at The Jockey Club, he was still connected to the long grapevine that passed-on inside tips, which he shared with his only grandchild, twenty-year-old Gesuela, or Jesse, as everyone called her. They often pooled their money to share racing bets, an activity that her parents tolerated with tacit disapproval, the occasional welcome windfall satisfying Jesse's seemingly never-ending need to buy art supplies that her parents otherwise funded. What her parents didn't know about, however, was their regular, illegal betting on team sports' games.

BACK IN THE kitchen, the culinary activity was in high gear, as were the spirits of the friends, or 'The Knights of San Lorenzo' as they called themselves. It was Frank who suggested the nickname, reasoning that their ritual meeting place, the St. Lawrence Market, was aptly named as St. Lawrence, in Italian, San Lorenzo, was the patron saint of cooks.

"So, tell us Frank, how did it happen that Lorenzo is the patron saint of cooks?" Javi asked, as he finished the peppers and moved on to the warm olives in white vermouth.

"San Lorenzo? He was a deacon of the early Church in Rome under Pope St. Sixtus, martyred during a pagan persecution led by the prefect of Rome who was after the church's wealth. Lorenzo rendered not the loot unto 'Caesar', distributing it to the poor instead, and then offered them to the prefect as their treasure, which earned him a slow roasting alive on a grate over an open fire, a torture he bore with incredible fortitude.

"He was reported to remark during his immolation, 'This side's done now; you can turn me over'. Thus, he became the patron saint of cooks," Frank concluded.

"Seems more like the patron saint of comedians; is that where 'roasting' someone at a banquet came from?" teased Paul.

"Wow, Paul, d'ya think that's a double entendre?" chuckled Javi.

"No, just a lame joke," Paul retorted.

"Anyway, his attributes are a grill and a braid of garlic," continued Frank, returning his attention to preparing the eggplant. "His feast day is August tenth."

"One more top-up of that delightful spumante,

Javi and I'm outta' here before Il professore hands me a spoon and an apron," exclaimed Lidia, who was lazily perched at the island across from Javi on the 'knock-off' Eames stool.

"No, the muse must never toil, only inspire," Javi's pompous declaration being punctuated by the festive pop of a newly opened bottle.

"No more work today, cara?" Nick asked.

"Absolutely not. I've put in a full Saturday morning and half this afternoon lining-up the assignments for *Your Best Life's* holiday edition. I need a little down time now.

"An editor over-working a theme is as bad as a painter overworking a canvas; the focus becomes muddled and ultimately lost. The trick is to know when to stop." This was a surprising declaration from Lidia, the driven professional.

"Well, I'm glad to hear it, I haven't seen much of you since you were made editor," lamented Nick, who rarely complained of his wife's long hours; he knew when she decided to accept the position that the magazine would be a jealous lover.

When they first met in Rome, Nick, eight years Lidia's senior, was an associate professor on the tenure track, she was an ambitious, assistant protocol advisor in the Canadian Embassy in Rome. They fell in love at first sight and were quickly married. Nick was content, as long as her passion was as equally invested in their marriage as it was in her career, although it was rumored there was plenty of playing around at the embassy, another reason he was glad they decided to come home.

And after all, the academic life was not without its temptations, long hours, stress, and commitments. To say nothing of the travel required to do primary research, present papers at conferences and hold summer courses abroad. But they kept their marriage together where many had not. Nick would've liked more children yet understood Lidia's position that more maternity leave would set her back professionally, and being a stay-at-home mom just wasn't her métier.

Well, it's better to have an accomplished wife than an aggrieved one, thought Nick, as the spice grinder finished its job on Javi's fresh and fragrant coriander seeds. Immediately Nick lifted off the lid, the sweet fragrance of their volatile oils hit the air "Ah, manna!" he declared, inhaling deeply. "The House of Israel called thy name; and it was like coriander seed, white; and the taste of it was like wafers made with honey: Exodus 16:31," he recited, only slightly feigning rapture.

"Now who sounds like a priest?" Frank protested.

"Okay then, let me turn from the sacred to the

profane; these potent little wonders here," in Nick's square, meaty palm, nestled several round dry white seeds, "are said by the ancients to possess aphrodisiac powers enhancing a man's virility. I have it on good authority from *The Arabian Nights*, among other sources. Conversely, in the Middle Ages, to slip a sachet of it beneath the marriage bed would ensure a wife's fidelity," he advised, returning his treasure to the spice jar.

"What about the husband's fidelity?" scoffed Lidia.

"Not so important as a wife's, cara. The issue being of primogenitor, and ensuring that the family silver, to say nothing of the family's estate goes to a rightful heir and kinsmen and not a stranger or rival," Nick expounded.

"Oh yes, and always a 'rightful heir' of the male variety no doubt," Lidia retorted, arching her back defensively.

"Usually, but mine is only to enlighten, not to challenge, that's *your* territory my dear feminist," Nick demurred.

"No, eh? Well, if I got you, Nero Ponti in the ring you wouldn't last one round!" declared Lidia, who was enjoying this friendly sparring with her husband, something they engaged in occasionally, matching their diverse, but not unequal wits.

"Oh mercy!" cried Nick, rolling his eyes in mock horror to the delight of their audience, who always felt at ease in the Ponti household, their hosts being a couple who could successfully set the tone of a gathering, and well-entertain their friends.

Nick turned his attention to the sauce, giving it the final blessing of a pinch of coriander, then left it to simmer gently for an hour, during which time he would help Frank roll out and cut the fresh pasta. Paul moved on to the panna cotta, aiming to have it set in the fridge before the arrival of his wife Becky, who managed to turn up early.

Becky was thirty-eight, three years younger than Lidia, tall, lean and athletic-looking; breezily casual, but not careless of her appearance, letting a few silver strands weave their way through the loose ringlets of her golden-red 'lob'. She had chalk white skin, and her nutmeg-brown freckles, no longer a source of chagrin, were generously sprinkled across her straight, refined nose, and high cheekbones.

The only redhead curse she still corrected were the pale eyebrows and eyelashes framing her green, amber-flecked eyes; those she had tinted a glossy mink-brown, a concession to high-maintenance vanity.

༄

"Hi Becky, c'mon in," Lidia greeted her friend at the front door. "Here give me your things," she said, extending a hand toward Becky, who slipped off her new, grey, combed mohair, wrap-coat.

"Ooh! This is really nice, looks great on you," Lidia said, as she stroked the soft, silver fox collar.

"Thanks Lidia, but the kids gave me so much grief over it!" Becky said as she unzipped her boots. "I told them that this fox, like the chickens we eat, are farmed for our use, which just made it worse. Danielle even threatened to become a vegan," Becky laughed.

"I know! You can't win," Lidia sighed, shaking her head, as she led her guest to the kitchen.

"Hi hon! You're early…Danielle still at the showroom?" Paul asked, giving Becky a peck on her cheek.

"No, Kate decided she wanted to earn a few brownie points, and relieved me for the last two hours so I could change and beat the traffic. Is that Bolognese sauce I smell?"

"Correct! Give the lady a drink Javi," Nick said.

"It's okay, I'll get it," Becky replied, reaching for one of the flutes near the bottle on the island. She poured herself a drink, then after taking a few sips, said, "This is very nice, but what's that fruity taste?"

"It's lychee, gives it a nice, exotic nose too," Lidia answered, inhaling the aroma of a freshly poured glass. "Oh yes, this is good. But some food would be good too, are you hungry Becky?"

"Starving, the showroom was so busy today, I didn't have time for lunch."

"Me neither. So how about it guys, can us hard-working women have something to hold us over 'til dinner?" Lidia asked, raising her eyebrows at Nick.

"Okay! Javi, get the antipasti platters together before Lidia jumps the island and bites a chunk outta me."

Javi pulled the platters and small plates from the top cabinet shelf, as Becky settled-in beside Lidia, watching him impatiently, as he began artfully arranging the food.

"I love this cheese," Lidia said, filching two pieces from the platter, handing one to her friend.

"Yes, it's got a nice nuttiness, then you get that little punch of pepper. I don't understand why Parmesan is so trendy, pecorino's got loads more taste," Becky said, reaching for some more, as Javi tried to slap her hand. "Ha-ha! Too fast for you, big boy." Becky laughed as she popped another piece of cheese into her mouth.

"Hey, can the cooks have some too?" Frank asked.

"Okay, okay, I'm nearly finished. Sheesh, I only have two hands and one has to fend off these two thieves," exclaimed Javi, nodding in the direction of Lidia and Becky.

Just as Lidia got up to pass around the napkins, and everyone took a little pause to eat, while Javi opened a bottle of sagrantino, Aldo emerged from the sitting room, complaining.

"Why didn't anybody call me?"

"No need, dad. I know you can, even through walls, detect the presence of food," Lidia laughed.

"Very funny. I don't know why, but every time I get a cold, my appetite doubles," he said, grabbing a few slices of salami and cheese.

"Yeah, but the question is where do you put it all? You never seem to gain an ounce," Lidia wondered, poking him in the ribs.

"I know. But you're just like me, the Campaniles are slim. Filly's side though, all plump. Your mom used to fight her weight, always counting the calories. But I like voluptuous women, they're sexy." Aldo grinned, taking a bite of salami.

Temporarily satiated, she and Becky headed to the dining room to lay the table. They set each place with Lidia's white china plates, then salad bowls of rose-colored Depression glass, and for pasta dishes, mixed transfer-ware flea market finds that added a touch of fun and whimsy.

The wine glasses were clear-glass balloons, the water tumblers of the same rose-glass as the salad bowls. Along the table's length Lidia placed several tea lights in cut-glass holders.

"I think that'll do," Lidia said, standing back regarding the table, as Becky lit the last tea light. "Now, let's see how dinner's going".

"Hope we eat soon. I'm so tired, and need to be up early tomorrow, promised to take Danielle skiing in Collingwood, although I'd rather have a lie-in," Becky said, following Lidia back to the kitchen, where the first course was ready to be served.

As dinner progressed through the first of five courses, conversation flew from food and wine, to politics, movies, celebrity gossip, landing with the panna cotta and grappa, on real estate.

Javi was extolling the location and amenities of his latest condo purchase and plans for upgrades. "Becky, I'd like you to look over the new place. I really need to get the builder's ugly crap outta there, as I may not flip this one. I think it'll be home for a few years. So, let me know when you can come over and bring some samples, I'm thinking distressed wood, wide plank?" Javi suggested.

"Well, the distressed look is certainly current, but I can't get out of the showroom, so why don't you come down and we'll discuss it. Bring some pictures and please bring the specs Javi, saves time, you may have lots of it, but I don't," Becky said, pushing her chair out, taking her dessert plate to the kitchen.

Paul looked at Javi, a little embarrassed by his wife's brusque response. "Sorry Javi, she's just had a long day. It's been crazy busy at the showroom and the kids just can't put in the hours now it's end of term. But don't worry, we'll get you sorted soon."

LATER THAT EVENING, Lidia prepared herself for bed, performing the ritual brushing of her glossy hair, smoothing on her porcelain skin and down her long neck, the mysterious elixir which held the dubious promise of eternal youth, being irresistible even to cynical feminists. She reviewed the evening's discourses.

"Nick," she addressed her husband already in bed, propped-up with what she thought hogged too many of their pillows. He was ensconced in a book, his late-night jazz program playing softly in the background. "Do you think Paul and Becky are alright?"

"Well...yes," he replied, reluctant to give the question his full attention.

"It's just that Becky seemed a bit grumpy during dinner and frankly, looked very unhappy."

"Unhappy? No, she's just tired, likely from the pressures of working in the business while trying to keep those three girls on track. Probably needs a couple of weeks away. Things will get better once Kate graduates from college, and the twins start full-time in the business," Nick said, knowing it was now futile to feign disinterest.

"Speaking of business," Lidia pursued, "it must be pretty good for them. Becky didn't seem too anxious for Javi's business; in fact, she put him off, telling him to come to the showroom. She knows Javi gets a nosebleed just thinking of travelling further north than Eglinton, never mind go to the wilds of Willowdale," laughed Lidia.

"They know how to handle Javi, remember the run-around he gave Paul with the flooring for the first unit he reno'd? I want cherry, no, walnut, no cancel that-everything bleached oak! It nearly broke-up their friendship."

Nick continued, "Javi is just playing the field at this point, seeing who's the most anxious for his business, who he can get the best deal from. At the end of the day, he knows he'll get the best product and work from Paul and Becky, who'll wait until Javi becomes impatient, wanting everything done a.s.a.p., then extract a dividend to 'put on the rush'. It's a little dance, they do it every time."

"I guess you're right," Lidia conceded. "Anyway, it seems that our Frank is enjoying teaching the Religion course at the Faculty of Education. I'm glad you put in a good word on his behalf, parish work certainly has its demands, but I don't think it engages his intellect."

"Yes, I know, with the company of dusty tomes, in haunted reading rooms is where he'd be most happy, but being a parish priest, beyond it pleasing his over-bearing mother, must have held an attraction," Nick chuckled.

"But Frank is committed to sacrifice in service, even though he's charming and handsome, a catch for the right woman, he chose a celibate life…" Lidia mused, as she slathered the luscious Italian bergamot hand cream between her fingers, on each side of her hands, extending to her slender wrists.

"Well, bella, in any case, he's a good priest. Now, if we've straightened-out our friends, may I get back to the fascinating facts in my reading?" Nick pleaded.

"What 'fascinating facts' can there be in, *In Bad Taste*? And what a strange choice of bedtime reading; it's such a creepy little book, researching 'delicacies' like cat-poop coffee and rotten cheese rife with live wriggling maggots. Yuck! Just imagine," she shuddered.

"Yes, just *imagine*," teased her husband.

BOEUF BOURGUIGNON

A BRILLIANT SHAFT of mid-winter, late afternoon sun, streamed through the ancient single glazing, illuminating the cramped office of Professor Nick Ponti, his leonine head caught in its beam, lolling lazily against his broad chest. In a moment he would begin to snore, sliding beneath a heavy blanket of fatigue. But the two abrupt raps on his half-open door made him quickly shrug-off slumber's cozy fleece.

Recovering his bearings, he greeted the tardy intruder with the semblance of a present mind; "You're a half-hour late, *Tahra*" –*or was it Teara? He couldn't remember which blonde-haired, blue-eyed undergrad he was addressing, they all seemed so 'much of a muchness'; their insistence on the particular pronunciation of their names, it seemed to him as a pretense to distinction. Tahra or Teara? Who cares how the two most banal syllables in the English language are pronounced? Tiramisu, or no, Tara-Mi –Su, now that's distinctive... sounds oriental! He chuckled inwardly at his own silly joke.*

"Uh, it's T*ea*ra, actually...and yeah, I'm sorry, but I was held-up with some heavy research in the stacks; just lost track of time," replied the undergrad, with a curt smile.

"Hmm, right," *held-up twittering at Starbucks, more like.* "Well now, T*ea*ra you wanted to discuss your last paper?" Nick swiveled his chair to face the girl.

"Yeah, um I don't really get why, given all the effort I put into that essay, you gave me such a low grade," she began, sliding edgewise into the proffered seat.

"I can't judge the effort you say is invested in this paper Tara, only the result, which *earned* fifty-two percent out of a possible one hundred," responded Nick.

"Yes, professor, we have established that the grade is unsatisfactory," she retorted, her diction and bearing becoming slightly imperious. "But what I don't understand is, why?"

"I refer you to my comments throughout your paper, and particularly those at the end." He matched her attitude, and determined to regain the upper hand, ratcheted it up a notch. "To wit; 'The thesis is supported by little research that does not go beyond the syllabus. The content is derivative, lacking depth of thought or original insights'," he quoted from his copy of the lack-luster work. "Ergo Tara, critical analysis, where is it? I know what Erwin Panofsky's theory of the three strata of subject matter and how to find meaning in a work of art is, but what do *you* think about it?" challenged Nick.

"Are you implying that I plagiarized that paper?" her voice, along with her color, rising.

"No, no it's not strictly speaking a question of plagiarism, you have quite properly provided footnotes and a bibliography in the accepted manner, but no originality of thought. Look, what does that poster say?" He pointed to a yellowed posting with frayed corners on the opposite wall.

"History tells us not all that was, merely all that was left," she read aloud, shrugging her shoulders.

"Exactly, so what history needs Tara, are bright young minds like yours to see what the 'old dead white guys' saw, then open *your* eyes, look at what they left, but *see* something different and relevant to *now*."

"What? You expect me, and the rest of the class to go one better than Panofsky?" she declared, leaning into the exchange.

"No, not better, simply different. Didn't you indicate on your profile sheet that you took the International Baccalaureate in Italy at Cambrian College? Surely you were taught critical textual analysis?"

"Well, yeah, but the thing is, I couldn't finish, I got mononucleosis and had to return home," she sulked, lowering her eyes.

"Oh dear, well nevertheless, advanced senior secondary education provides this instruction as well and it is expected at this level," he concluded rising, hoping that would wrap-up this tedious exchange.

"But can't I do a make-up paper?" she pleaded, now from an inferior, seated position.

"No, I'm sorry, it's against department policy, take more time with the next paper to think deeply, look carefully and be inspired, I'm sure you are full of it." He couldn't resist sneaking in a little ribbing as he gathered his papers in his briefcase.

"What do you mean, 'full of it'?" she challenged, a little uncertainly.

"Why Tara, inspiration of course. Have a good weekend."

She rose and turned toward the door, "Yeah, right, and a good weekend to you, *'professor'*," she shot back insolently, as if his credentials were suddenly in question.

God! Sometimes I really hate this job, dealing with unprepared, lazy, or simply unsuited students and the even worse plague, their pushy, 'helicopter parents', he thought morosely. Not only was he tired, but now must endure the subway rush-hour crush he had hoped to avoid by leaving a little early. Oh well, home was only a thirty-minute ride away. There he could light the fire, listen to the divine 'Miss Ella' Fitzgerald, and quaff a little Côtes du Rhône while warming-up last night's boeuf Bourguignon, then snooze in his favorite wing chair until Lidia returned from her Friday night meeting.

Yes, a nice quiet night in was what he needed. Aldo was at the club playing cards with his friend, Cheech. Jesse was wherever her art group, The Paper Dolls, were committing a new act of art, dumpster-diving, or partying with other student artists, probably somewhere at a bar in the now artsy Junction area; Queen St. West having become too expensive and too gentrified, losing its 'boho' edge.

However, as he approached his back gate from the alley, having taken the short cut from the subway across the park, Nick was surprised to see the Honda parked on the brick pad they had created for the purpose, giving-up some of their precious garden space to avoid the hassle of permit parking on the street. Jesse must be home he thought; they were a one car family, Lidia and he both worked a short subway ride from downtown where parking was difficult and expensive, so their daughter, having the farthest commute to York University, used the car most days and weeknights when her parents didn't need it.

He could smell the Bourguignon from the back porch as he dropped his things on the parson's bench, hung-up his coat and went to the kitchen, greeting his daughter with a peck on both her rosy, round cheeks, just as she made to set the table.

"Not out with 'The Dolls' tonight Jess?"

The Paper Dolls was a group of art students whose chief preoccupation was salvaging used, surplus billboards, printed matter, and other oddments from industrial and commercial sources, some of it from a depot called Arts Junktion, where they could get material for free, then create installations, photographing them for their website and sometimes cadging the odd commission to do display windows for local avant-garde designers.

"Nope, I have to finish a paper for Monday, so I thought I'd keep you company, you lucky guy." Jesse smiled at her hungry father.

"Mooch-off me, more like. And there better be enough in this pot for two, greedy guts," he said, lifting the lid and giving the contents a little stir to check the meat wasn't sticking to the bottom.

"Don't panic dad, there's enough there for four – and I warn you, I do plan on having seconds. I just love it the next day, it's always better then; I wonder why that is?" she asked, turning to hand her father a glass of wine.

"Well, boeuf Bourguignon is like marriage, you start out as distinct individuals, just like the main elements in the stew, then become more 'as one' over time as you undertake the sullen endeavor of life 'ensemble'. Marriage doesn't happen at the altar, you know, that's only where the intent takes form."

"Hmm, so it's like off passion's hot boil, then into life's cold fridge. Sure sounds like a drag to me," Jesse scoffed.

"Not at all, you'll find out some day, but not too soon, eh?" Nick ruffled his daughter's long, curly, chestnut locks.

"I haven't met anyone yet I'd trust my life with dad," Jesse said, smoothing down her hair. "So no, I'm not interested in being tied-down."

As he loaded the last dirty fork into the dishwasher, Nick mused about his young, talented offspring. He felt happy and content to have her living at home, albeit in their basement apartment, which was okay as he knew most college students, like moths, avoid the light of day, being driven in the wee hours to the neon of the nearest aptly named, Starbucks.

He felt that it was strange so many of his colleagues were eager to kick their fledglings out of the nest after high school, as he liked having Jess and her young friends around, just as he liked having his father-in-law, Aldo with them.

Nick lost his birth family when he was very young, his hard-working, immigrant father, Antonio, dropping dead of a heart attack when Nick was five. Two years later, while visiting her cousin in Rochester, his mom, Viviana met and impetuously married Alf, a local bar owner. And that was the end of family life for young Nick Ponti.

The long and irregular hours they kept as bar owners were not conducive to bringing-up a young child, his mother and stepfather reasoned, so arrangements were made for Nick to board in Toronto with her brother and sister-in-law who were childless, just until the time came when he was old enough to join them.

But that time never came. Except for a few weeks in the summers, when he was old enough to be a busboy at the restaurant, and sometimes at Christmas, as that was their busy season, these were the times, with few exceptions, when he saw his mom and stepdad Alf, who was nice enough to him, but somewhat indifferent, having no children of his own and little interest in raising someone else's.

His material needs were more than adequately met from his father's estate and his mother's monthly support cheques. They provided well for his upkeep and education, provisions which did not inhibit the rest of the family from looking upon him with pity, referring to him, some even to this day, as 'poor Nick'.

He couldn't say that he wasn't cared for, it was just that the effort his guardians invested in his upbringing was circumscribed by their fastidious attention to religious observance, social propriety, domestic order, and discipline, but was not extended to displays of approval, encouragement, or affection.

So it was, that being accepted into the St. Michael's choir school was his salvation from loneliness, no more an outsider, he now had the refuge and solace of the dignity that it conferred on its young members, marking them as gifted, and the camaraderie that singing, studying, and playing together with like-minded boys offered.

Finally, he belonged, and was soon informally adopted by the gregarious extended family of his best friend Javi, often spending holidays and weekends with them. Nick became accepted as a permanent fixture in their frenetic household.

Like the other children, he was never made a fuss over or particularly noticed, just indiscriminately spoiled, rebuked and pressed into any domestic service required by Javi's mother, Imelda. She had seven children whose names she could never remember accurately, often mistaking Javi for Jesu or Jesu for Juan Carlos and was vaguely confused when the nanny's headcount upon arriving at a destination yielded one or two extra faces, she'd mutter herding them ahead, "Never mind nana, better one too many than one too few."

When Nick was seventeen, his mother succumbed to breast cancer and they held her funeral in Toronto. At the wake Nick, Javi, Frank and Paul sang the *In Paradisum* in Latin, and all the old people cried. Immediately afterwards, Nick and his friends tried sneaking-out with his older cousins to the neighboring pool hall, but his vigilant aunt collared them before they could escape out the back.

Later, at the restaurant, the boys were given rounds of fiery grappa by Carlo, Nick's godfather. Nick was sick in the car going home, his aunt and uncle shaking their heads in silent disgust. The following Monday, he gladly returned to his studies, eventually graduating with honors. He never saw or heard from his stepfather again, and he tacitly refused to visit his mother's grave; his aunt finally gave-up telling him he should.

BURNING THE MIDNIGHT OIL?

"Where's dad?" Lidia inquired of her snoozing husband, trying to rouse him with an annoying jostle of his arm. "Hey, you, wake-up... time to go to bed Nick, it's twelve-thirty! And where's dad, did he call for a ride?" her urgency being not so much motivated by concern for her tardy father, who was likely 'sleeping it off' at Cheech's, as it was to focus attention away from her own late arrival.

"What? I don't know where Aldo is. If he called, I would've heard it," said Nick, rubbing his eyes and stretching his neck. "Hey, what time is it? How come *you're* so late?"

"Never mind that," retorted Lidia, feigning annoyance, "I should call Cheech, just to make sure the old reprobate's there." She made a show of punching-in the numbers on the keypad, making-out that the responsibility always fell to her capable hands, which regularly picked-up the slack for her lazy spouse. Nothing, they both knew, could be further from the truth.

"No, no just leave it, Lidia. I'm sure they're both asleep."

"Oh alright, I guess he's okay," she conceded, putting her phone away. "Just wish he'd call to let us know."

At that, Nick rose stiffly from the cocoon of his wing chair and headed upstairs where he would exchange its comfort for that of his cozy bed, making a mental note for the next morning to pursue the inquest of his wife's late arrival, a note he typically failed to recall.

ELEVENES

SATURDAYS IN THE Ponti household were usually reserved for work, Nick at his courses, Lidia at her column. By 11:30 a.m. Nick found himself in need of a little repast and set about making-up a tray with a roundel of buttery St. Paulin cheese, a small terrine of homemade chicken liver paté; a flat bread-carta musica with fennel seed, Lidia's favorite; membrillo, and two tumblers of pinot gris he intended to share with his wife, ensconced with her laptop, in the nook of the sun-filled bay window on the second floor.

"Cara, take a break, I've made us elevenses," Nick shouted.

"Good! I sure can use it," she responded, stretching her arms and yawning. She descended to the sitting room where her thoughtful husband had placed their snack on the coffee table, between the sofa and the love seat.

"Cin-cin," they chimed together, raising their glasses to drink.

"God, I needed that! I despair of post-modern society, Nick, I really do. Get this, I have a tweet-battle going on, some from guests, others from hosts, on the question of whether or not you should be allowed to bring *children* to a cocktail party."

"Really? How bizarre," exclaimed Nick, cutting into the soft, luscious cheese.

"The guests are aggrieved when their hosts decline their request, or that there is no provision made for the entertainment of children whose parents don't even have the manners to ask if they can bring them along.

"The parents' reason that this is unfair, as how are their kids going to learn to behave at such events if they don't experience them now," Lidia said, rolling her eyes, continued. "Well, I can tell you that little Sid and Nancy will certainly need to look outside their home for role models if their parents are so socially clueless.

"Anyway, what ten-year-old needs to know how to handle herself at a cocktail party? Perhaps when she will actually be called upon to use this skill, in twenty years' time, there may not even be such things as cocktail parties; one can only hope."

"So, not having a good day then?" Nick chuckled.

"Very perceptive Nick…and you?"

"Me? I'm having great fun writing-up my annual Christmas-exam review lecture."

"Is that the one where you deliver a lecture full of inaccuracies and misinformation?" asked Lidia, arching an eyebrow.

"That's right, 'Fact or Fabrication?' Where the students, divided into teams must spot the lies, then each team has a crack at correcting them. The freshmen class loves it. I'm rather proud of it this year. For example, listen and see if you can spot the fabrications;

'It is well-known that Pico della Mirandola's existentialist ideas influenced such mannerist painters as Botticelli and Giambologna…well?"

"Well, what?" Lidia asked, distracted, cutting a thin slice of some tart, membrillo.

"Can you spot the fabrications? There are no less than four, for God's sake!" exclaimed Nick.

"Really, how fascinating, now is there any more carta musica?" Lidia reached into the basket only to find Nick had consumed the last one.

"You don't take a blind bit of interest in my

work, do you?"

"Of course, I do. But you're supposed to be edifying young minds, not confusing them. I mean, do you really call that education?" Lidia admonished her exasperated husband.

Nick sighed, as he got up to fetch more flat bread, deciding to bring the half bottle of pinot back too.

"Hi Jess," Nick greeted his daughter as she walked-in the front door. "Come and join us, I'll get you a glass. Are you just getting in?"

"Yeah, I stayed at Athina's last night and I'm starving!" Jesse plopped down beside her mother.

"Doesn't that girl ever eat? She's so thin, gorgeous eyes, but too thin," pronounced Lidia as she spread some cheese on the crisp flat bread, shattering the edges, loosing a flurry of crumbs onto her lap.

"Oh, mom," Jesse moaned, licking some paté from her fingers, an act she knew irritated Lidia. "Why must you always critique my friends' appearance? Athina is five foot ten, for god's sake, and always, since grade six, had a hard time keeping-on weight, you *know* that".

"Well, living on yogurt and muesli doesn't help. And I don't critique peoples' appearance, I just notice aesthetics. I'm a very visual person, where do you think you get your talent in art from?" Lidia retorted.

"Well certainly *not* from you, mom," Jesse sniffed. "I don't care if people's looks conform to some arbitrary, anorexic, standard of beauty imposed on women by misogynist ad men and gay designers, I care about what's visually interesting and complex, not what's deemed as being merely beautiful," Jesse pronounced disdainfully.

"Speaking of designers," Lidia said, carefully steering the conversation away from this ages-old argument she knew she couldn't win. "How would you like to join me, and Kate at the Gaia Gurl trunk show two weeks on Sunday? Anne got us invites, so I want to buy both of you something nice for Christmas from their spring line."

"Only if they do some stuff in hemp and Kate comes for *sure*," Jesse said, grabbing the last carta musica, heading down the hallway to her basement flat.

"You know Nick, if that kid didn't look so much like you, I'd swear she was a changeling."

SACK CLOTH AND ASHES

LIDIA WAS MORE than happy to sink into the back seat of the family's Honda and let her god daughter,

Kate, drive as she was a whiz at parallel parking. Jesse rode shotgun, on the look-out for an empty parking spot near The Bay's new event space, The Arcadian, the trunk show's venue.

"Look, just up ahead Kate, that guy's pulling-out." Jesse motioned ahead to her right.

"Yes, come on grandddaddy, that's it, turn the wheel," encouraged Kate. "No, don't bother looking in the rear-view to see if your Brylcreem's holding-up, just wipe your nose… oh no, not on your sleeve…oh, yuck!"

Both girls groaned in revulsion, slightly louder than necessary, as Kate in one swift, deft motion, pulled next to the curb, occupying the spot.

"Good job, Kate, but I really could've done without the blow-by-blow." Lidia laughed, swinging her shapely legs out from the open door, emerging with her usual grace.

"Well, we're off to see the wizard," she chirped, linking arms with both girls as they briskly walked the short block to their destination.

Since they were a bit late, there was little more than standing room left, nevertheless Lidia found a perch on a bench at the back of the room and motioned for the girls to join her. She scanned the crowd, but couldn't see her friend, Anne, who was likely still in New York.

As the mimosas and canapés were passed around, Jesse and Kate chatted, while Lidia quietly assessed the renovated space. She couldn't help but feel sad over the contemporary incarnation of the former Arcadian Court, a once elegant and spacious, 1920's Art Deco dining room with forty-foot ceilings.

Its sparkling Lalique crystal chandeliers were replaced with plebian glass fixtures, the mezzanine's ornate, wrought iron railings removed, in their stead, tempered glass panels-the kind in high-rise balconies. The graceful sweep of arched windows, now blind to their once expansive view of the downtown skyline. Gone too was the grand piano always playing in reception; the numerous tables, laid with thick, white linen cloths and heavy silver cutlery, mere ghosts.

The Arcadian Court was where Lidia's mother took her every year as a birthday treat, post shopping-spree in the adjacent department-store complex. After buying a new outfit and shoes for Lidia, mother and daughter would lunch in style, amid the wealthy Rosedale and Forest Hill matrons, often accompanied by private-school blazered, grandchildren. They always ordered their favorite, chicken pot pie, for which the restaurant was famous.

But on Lidia's twelfth birthday, she announced she'd rather have the money to go to the new mall, eat Chinese food with her friends, and choose her own outfit. Her mother balked, suggesting, "You can ask Donna to come with us. Then we could see a movie after lunch, any movie you like!"

Lidia was firm, she wanted no part of her mother picking out her clothes, especially in the presence of her best friend, then go to lunch surrounded by a bunch of blue-haired old biddies. So, she got her way. Lidia found herself tearing-up a little at the memory, *I shouldn't have been so mean, she just wanted me to herself for a few more years, now I wish I'd had more years like that with her, she and I, pretending to be grand ladies together, if only for a day.*

Lidia tamped her eyes with a tissue, took another sip of her mimosa and felt no comfort in being back in that room, which now looked like a soulless banquet hall, the kind you find near industrial malls. No matter, today she was here with her own daughter and wouldn't let someone else's bad taste ruin it for her.

Soon after the hip-hop pumped out of the sound system, the designer made her entrance, then the show began. The girls seemed to be interested and enjoying themselves, but Lidia found the unusual spring pallet of putty with the odd splash of orange and turquoise a little jarring and disliked the way the designer layered-on the various shapes and textures of the pieces on her zombie-looking models. The styling seemed to her indiscriminate, as if they were scrawny clothes-hangers heaped with rumpled laundry.

Oh well, she thought, at least there's no hemp. But that feeling of relief evaporated quickly as the next model stomped out wearing a slouchy, asymmetrical take on the classic trench coat in the loathsome fabric.

"Oh damn," she muttered. "Here come the sack cloth and ashes."

Jesse grimaced. "It's a very sustainable fiber mom, socially responsible and environmentally friendly."

"Oh, to hell with the environment! That garment looks and hangs like a gunny sack; anyway, we just drove here in a fossil-fueled four-wheel drive, didn't we?" Lidia shot back.

"Right, that's the one I want mom; what do *you* like Kate?" Jesse turned her back defiantly on Lidia and addressed her friend. Aware that this was a loaded question, Kate prevaricated for a few minutes, buying time until salvation arrived in the form of a line of formidable stick insects marching menacingly, leg over leg, single file down the catwalk – the accessories line.

And in virtuous, but quite attractive turquoise and orange fish-skin, they swung fish-skin totes, hooked their fingers in crisscrossed strings of skinny fish-skin belts and sneered blankly from the brims of smart fish-skin fedoras and flat newsboy caps.

"Oh Lidia, can I have one of those cool turquoise caps?" Kate exclaimed.

"Of course, if that's what you want, that turquoise will look fabulous with your red hair."

Relieved, Kate made for the hats to find one that fit, in the meantime, Lidia pulled her daughter aside and laid-down the law through clenched teeth. "Listen missy, I'm not going to plunk down hundreds of dollars so my disaffected daughter can schlep down the streets of Toronto looking like a sack of potatoes! If you want to look like a shapeless lump, just find an old piece of burlap while you're dumpster-diving and I'll be glad to run it up for you. Now, find something suitable… please."

Jesse glared at her mother, shook her arm loose, and directed her to 'get lost,' then bolted from the room.

"Where's Jesse?" asked Kate.

Lidia averted her eyes and lied, "Oh, she had to go, forgot she was supposed to meet someone…somewhere, so are we all set?"

"Oh, okay. Just hang-on a minute, I need to get this." Kate checked her text message, it was from Jesse warning her that Lidia was an evil witch who had sold her identical infant twin into white slavery and would gobble her-up, if the canapés ran out. Smirking, she quickly texted a commiserating missive back, then joined her waiting godmother.

"THANKS LIDIA," KATE said, kissing her lightly on the cheek before getting out of the car. "You know, Jesse's having a hard time just now," she offered reluctantly.

"Oh?"

"It's that guy she was seeing, you know, Ainsworth – the filmmaker? Well, it seems he's now seeing Athina; Jesse's really torn-up, didn't she tell you?" Kate was regretting her revelation.

"Oh sure." Lidia lied for the second time that day. "I just thought she'd gotten over it, but thanks, bella. Have a good Christmas and tell your mom and dad we'll see them New Year's Day, okay?"

Well, well, a boyfriend named Ainsworth, eh. What kind of name is Ainsworth? Lidia wondered, resolving to find out.

BLUEBERRY WAFFLE BLUES

CHRISTMAS FESTIVITIES WERE almost a week gone as Nick and Lidia sat facing each other across the kitchen island on a quiet Sunday morning sipping cappuccino and sharing *The New York* Times, she the Arts section, he the magazine.

Lidia paused to sip from the warm frothy brew, then silently appraised her husband who was deeply engaged in reading an article on playwright Clifford Odets.

Hm... he has a certain cuddly, curmudgeonly charm, she mused to herself, *even, with his 'bed head' and wearing that gnarly old sweater. He's so nice and solid; I never liked scrawny men.* She felt an urge to reach over and ruffle his hair.

Just then, Nick looked up quizzically, "Something on your mind, Lidia?"

"Oh, have you seen our daughter recently?" Lidia said, recovering herself.

"Well, my extra sensory powers of perception tell me that our ardent environmentalist is taking her usual twenty-minute Sunday morning shower, which means I'll have to wait until noon for mine," Nick grumbled.

"Ha ha, Kreskin. It's just that we haven't actually seen or talked to her since…"

"You mean since you and she had that very mature exchange over the purchase of a hemp coat?" reproached Nick.

"Come on now, she ate Christmas dinner with us, didn't she?"

"Oh yes, and then ran out like her pants were on fire," Nick rejoined.

"Well then, it's time we ended this sulk, let's entice her out of the 'bat cave' with some of your blueberry waffles and those horrible breakfast sausages you insist on buying."

"Perhaps you're right, we haven't had a nice family breakfast in ages, and I do feel like some waffles, so go ahead tell her, I can hear the shower's off now." He rose to begin preparation for he and Jesse's favorite feast.

"*Jeeess*," Lidia called down the basement stairs from the doorway off the kitchen. "Daddy's making your favorite blueberry waffles with maple syrup."

"I'm not hungry," she shouted brusquely.

"Oh, c'mon daddy'll be so disappointed, he even bought those greasy mystery-meat sausages you both like." Lidia laughed.

"Oh, alright! I'll be up in a minute," Jesse said, feigning annoyance.

"Well, she's coming," said Lidia to her husband's back as he rummaged in the fridge. "And don't say this snit is all my fault, Jess's been really sulky ever since the 'Ainsworth incident'."

"Ainsworth?" Nick said, raising his voice as he banged his head on the refrigerator shelf. "Who the hell is Ainsworth? And why haven't I been told about him?"

"Exactly," whispered Lidia. "That's what I want you to find out…who is he, how long was she seeing him, what does he do, who his people are etc…the whole nine yards, Nick!"

"What… aren't you going to be here?" Nick said, surprised.

"No, she won't open-up in front of me, anyway I told you I wanted to start spin class at the 'Y'. I reminded you yesterday, Nick."

"You did?"

"I most certainly did. Now I've got to go, or I won't make it." Lidia proffered her cheek for a goodbye kiss, which Nick obliged, then smiling to himself, decided not to wipe-off the adorable little bead of foam clinging to his wife's upper lip.

AFTER THE LAST waffle was shared and more sausages

consumed than were good for either of them, Nick pushed his plate aside, rested his chin on his hand and inquired of his sullen daughter, "So, you want to tell me why you're so glum?"

"Ah, so this is what the waffles were about," Jesse mused, passing a finger through the shallow slick of syrup left on her plate.

"Yes that, and 'just because', okay?" Nick gave her free hand an assuring pat.

"Well, it's like this; somebody I really liked and who I thought felt the same, let me down with somebody else I really trusted. So, I feel very angry and hurt at the moment," Jesse said quietly.

"And would the 'trusted somebody' be otherwise known to us as your best friend Athina and the other 'somebody' the mysterious heartbreaker, Ainsworth?"

"Yep, that's them, the Judas twins… and how do you know his name?"

"Mom told me," Nick said, picking-up their empty plates.

"Shit! How did she find out?"

"What? You're asking me? Your father, aka 'the last man to know' a status by the way, I plan on revising by hacking into your Face Book account."

"Sorry, dad, it must've been Kate who told her. How much does she actually know?"

"Not much, just that he's disappointed you and if I can't dish-out more when she returns, then you'll be squealing to the 'Grand Inquisitor' herself and believe me, she's oiled her thumb-screws." He laughed, hoping to lighten his daughter's mood.

"Oh, I've got it, good cop/bad cop, eh? Well, I'll spill, but just for you dad. I am not afraid of mom!"

"Course not, neither am I," affirmed Nick. They both lied, as much to reassure themselves as each other.

Jesse became animated as she told her father about Ainsworth. He and his family had emigrated in the seventies from the Caribbean Island of Martinique; he was a promising photographer and film maker. Then she explained how she came to work part-time for him as a technical assistant when her friend, Meghan, his model, and lover left upon discovering theirs wasn't an exclusive arrangement and how she herself briefly fell beneath his apparently potent spell.

Watching her enthuse about this man made it obvious to Nick that she still had a crush on him, a realization that made him feel at once embarrassed and protective of his vulnerable young daughter.

"Well, never mind, it seems like he's just playing the field, I doubt he'll last very long with Athina either." Nick gave Jesse a hug.

"Really, you think so?" she said, her face brightening, a glint of hope in her eyes. *Uh, oh,* thought Nick, *I don't think I should have said that.*

FOLLOW THE WINE!

ALDO SAT IN his tee-shirt by the window in his sitting room, watching the snowflakes make their indolent descent from the grey as gun-metal sky. His breath condensed in a halo on the pane interrupting his view; he ran two fingers in a streak across it, as if bestowing a blessing. But this was an absent-minded gesture, as his thoughts were far away, in a long-lost place of yearning.

After rapping lightly on the half-closed door, Lidia bustled in with a freshly ironed shirt. "Here dad, put it on now, our company is due soon. Aren't you cold sitting there by the window? Dad? What's the matter? Tell me," she implored.

"Ahh, it's nothing, just that New Year's seems to get me down. What's new in it for me, eh? Be honest, what do I have to look forward to?" Aldo responded listlessly.

"Oh, now," she whispered sitting down on the foot stool in front of him, placing her hands over his.

"You have health, your family, friends, life's not so bad, you know."

"But it's empty this life, there's nothing to plan and strive for, no challenges to rise to, no woman to make love to, no child to hold and dream a wonderful future for. It's just one day following another, no matter if it's Sunday, or Monday, one meal after another, one nightmare after another." He withdrew his hands and rubbed his eyes, offered a little smile to his worried daughter. "I'm sorry, I shouldn't be like this, spoiling your party."

"You haven't spoiled anything, everyone gets a little maudlin at this time of year, it's okay. Are you having those awful dreams again? Maybe you should see the doctor?" Lidia suggested.

"Ach, what can the doctor do about it, give me sleeping pills? I won't take pills. Forget it," Aldo said, straightening himself, making to stand.

"Well, then maybe you could do some volunteer work, to get out more, see new people. Why not go with Cheech on his visits to that retirement home?"

"I'll see, now go and get yourself ready. I'll be out in a minute and thanks for my shirt," he said, giving his daughter a peck on the cheek.

"My pleasure, dad. And don't worry, things will get better this year, just you wait and see." With that she left him to dress for brunch.

Since Nick and Javi had everything under control in the kitchen, Lidia had about twenty minutes to change into her new orange, ankle-length Missoni knit dress she cadged on Spadina for half its full retail. She paired it with soft-as-butter, beige suede ankle strap heels and the gold and amber tear-drop earrings Nick got her for Christmas. She carefully placed the vintage tortoise shell clip to secure her chignon and headed downstairs to the dining room.

Lidia was quite proud of this room in their 1890's brick semi. She had decorated it thoughtfully, creating an ambience of warmth and relaxation, but also of understated elegance, achieved mainly using reflective surfaces and a light, monochromatic palette on the walls and in the textiles, punctuated by original dark oak floors and millwork.

A large, colorful Persian carpet served as a visual anchor. Except for the hand-knotted carpet, color and pattern were restrained, using instead 'tone on tone' embossed textures in the soft furnishings and the judicious use of flattering ambient lighting, consisting mainly of vintage crystal and luster-ware pieces, creating a glamorous effect.

For this, their traditional New Year's Day brunch, Lidia chose a palette of white with a little green, a nod to the frosty season, betraying a hint of spring in the green accents in the floral arrangement, white roses, green skimmia and variegated ivy, large white napkins for the lap, layered with smaller green ones for the lips and fingers. The table runner was a length of green and white toile she had purchased as a remnant, then edged in green grosgrain ribbon, with matching green tassels at each of its four corners.

In the bay window, where the Christmas tree last stood, she placed a butler's table and a tall green glass vase filled with green and white kale. Another tall, imposing vase of fragrant white lilacs and a big silver bowl of perfect Granny Smith apples greeted their guests from the hall table.

Yes, she was very pleased with the effect, it was her contribution to their hospitality, an enhancement to the wonderful food her husband loved to prepare and share with their friends and family.

Lidia loved entertaining, the only thing she found irksome was the unfailing tendency of their guests to congregate in the kitchen, no matter how smart or casual the occasion, inexplicably they loved hanging-out there, amid the cooking smells, sounds and chaotic jumble of pots and pans.

Her colleague, Shelton Avery, wine columnist and professional misanthrope, once offered her a solution to the dilemma; "Please, it's simple; they follow the smell of food into the kitchen because they're hungry, but eventually, they get thirsty, so they will 'follow the wine'. Just stand in the kitchen doorway brandishing a bottle aloft 'like a strange device' and shout, 'anyone for a top-up, in the living room'? They'll follow the wine, slavering like the proverbial Pavlov's dogs."

She hated to admit it, but he did have a point. Instead of looking to Emily Post for guidance, she guessed she should consult Cesar Millan.

Ah..., she sighed to herself, *Shelton's so clever, easy on the eyes too,* Lidia was glad he could accept her invitation to brunch.

The brisk *brrring* of the doorbell shook her from her reverie, Lidia immediately went into 'hostess with the mostest' mode, taking coats, kissing cheeks, and beaming New Year's greetings; she was in her element. The guest list this year was 'the boys' and Aldo plus the quiet but congenial Becky. As for the rest, there was the witty Shelton, Anne the fashion buyer, world traveler and Lidia's long-time single friend. Then Nick's new friend from Istria, Gordan, a doctoral candidate; Lidia hoped they wouldn't end-up huddled in a corner, deep in gossip about college politics.

That made their number ten, not too many for the available space, bunching-up a little help break the ice, and not too few to let the conversation drag.

Lidia cared less about the boy-girl demographic when planning a party as she did to orchestrate the various personalities and interests of the company.

It also seemed to her that adhering to the b-g pattern left singletons out in the cold, or worse, feeling set-up; the whole occasion seeming nakedly contrived, conveying the message, 'get paired-off now, as your single status makes us feel uncomfortable'. Too much pressure, the mating opportunities were better left to a cocktail party where the gender line-up was less obvious, as people circulated.

WHEN ALL THE guests were seated, after the requisite herding from the kitchen and the Bollinger poured, Nick brought in a big silver tray laden with a bed of dill fronds and chipped ice supporting Malpeque oysters on the half shell with mignonette sauce. This was followed by Aldo's soused salmon, baskets of blinis, devilled quail's eggs topped with caviar, a white winter salad of grated celeriac and Belgian endive, followed by small bowls of stracciatella soup ladled over delicate enoki mushrooms and spring onions. Then the piece-de-resistance, homemade fettuccine with a champagne, butter and white truffle sauce, the truffles courtesy of Javi.

To end the elegant repast were Lidia's favorite, ouefs à la neige, or snow eggs, poached meringues sitting in a nest of spun sugar surrounded by a pool of velvety custard. Finally, there was espresso and iced amaro with lemon twists and a plate passed around of white chocolate truffles and pistachio cantucci.

The conversation, like the company, was lively and diverse, ranging from what were the chances of 'the gonads' as Torontonians irreverently and affectionately called their Toronto Argonauts, making it to the Grey Cup this season. Their beloved CFL football team was currently on a winning streak, predicted to beat their archrivals, the Hamilton Tiger-Cats, out of this year's play-offs, or so the assembled sports-wits pronounced, chief amongst them Aldo, who had brightened-up considerably and was game to set the odds.

By the time the salmon was served, the topic had moved-on to the astounding escalation in real estate prices; was it a bubble, if so when would it burst? And how would young people ever be able to move out of the parental home and into their own mortgages?

A top-up of wine and a lull in the conversation inspired Shelton to propose a toast to his hosts, praising the food and especially his colleague's beautiful table setting. Lidia smiled, saying that it was what she loved to do, then recounted how Jesse, demurring from helping her mother with the floral arrangements, called her 'Mrs. Dalloway'.

"Can you imagine? You'd think an art student would at least show some interest," Lidia exclaimed.

"Frankly, I find that encouraging," Nick retorted.

"Oh, and why's that?" asked Anne.

"Well, it means that my daughter's reading literature, Virginia Woolf no less and, not just those adult comic books," Nick scoffed.

"Graphic novels!" cried Gordan, "You can't get students away from them. I find this new genre silly and tedious, especially the illustrations."

"Anyway," rejoined Lidia. "I hate to burst your bubble, Nero, it's more likely that she saw the film, than actually read the book."

The talk then focused on the young off-spring of the assembled. Anne asked, "How are Kate and Jess making out, I haven't seen them in ages. Have they made plans for after graduation?"

"They're good, and loved the trunk show, thanks." Becky said. "They've joined an art group called The Paper Dolls. They've even been in a few group-shows and done some fashion display design."

"Yeah, and on the strength of that work and her personal portfolio, Kate's going to grad school next year," Paul interjected, proudly.

"Wonderful, congratulations to her Paul," offered Anne. Then turning to her hostess, "And my god daughter, Lidia? What are her plans?"

Nick was quick to answer for her, "Oh, Jesse's going to Teachers' College. She's a natural pedagogue."

"At first, she considered doing her masters, eventually aiming at curatorial work. But then she and Nick did some research and eventually decided teaching was the best choice," Lidia affirmed.

"Right now though, she and Kate have taken a pot of chili, some bread and god knows what else to their 'Occupy Toronto' group's New Year strategy meeting. I know they're being socially conscious and politically proactive but risking arrest at a rowdy protest is something else," Nick said.

"Don't worry, it's a rite of passage for them, this is a different generation from yours, security isn't uppermost in their minds right now. Canadians aren't as politicized as their European cousins who have been reared in a more politically volatile environment; it's time for them to catch-up," Gordan asserted.

"Easy for you to say, Gordan, although I know your people have been through hell in the Baltic wars, but once you become a parent, you can't help but worry about the safety of your kids, that's your job," Nick retorted.

"Point taken," conceded Gordan.

"Nevertheless," Lidia added, "I don't think this is really a 'political rite of passage'. Young people don't always bother to vote. The 'Occupy Bay Streeter's' didn't even know what they wanted, much less understand the real impact of the 2008 crash on those whose retirement savings have been eviscerated. To say nothing of the government's position that we have to work longer."

"The well-pensioned Health and Welfare Minister constantly harps on that as we age, we'll be a *drain* on the system. We, the ones who lost the most, paid the most taxes are now vilified to the young by our government in the press," Shelton protested passionately.

Paul, shouting a spontaneous, "Here, here!" was accompanied by dessert spoons chiming against the side of the crystal, breaking the somber intensity of the moment.

"Politics and the economy aside, I think all this over-earnest environmentalism is a symptom of the young raised in a secular society. Taking care of the environment's become the new religion," observed Frank.

Becky broke in with, "I get tired of the guilt trip

when I fail to immaculately rinse out the recycling. My kids act like leaving no carbon footprint is the path to post-modern sainthood."

"I know. We raised our daughter in a perfectly good religion; I'm surprised she doesn't practice it instead. Even as a child she was possessed of an unnerving piety," Lidia observed.

"Now cara," Nick admonished.

"Oh, c'mon Nick," said Lidia, slightly tipsy now. "Remember when she was eight and got hold of some Carr's crackers and dad's Chianti, then proceeded to administer Holy Communion to the neighborhood kids? At first, I couldn't understand why they were rolling around our yard acting like little lunatics, until they started puking in the flower beds," she grumbled into her glass, taking a sip of champagne. Suddenly, she snorted with laughter at the image, sputtering out the bubbly, making everyone else laugh too; levity defeating gravity.

Chapter Two

SPRING

Even though Aldo had initially balked at accompanying Cheech on his 'old folks' visits, harboring a secret superstition that spending too much time in an assisted living residence was marking his own card. Eventually he relented, appreciating the value of the interaction to his new acquaintance, feeling useful in providing Tony Assunta a connection to the larger world. And much as a plain girl can feel downright pretty beside an ugly one, ironically and a little uncharitably, Aldo felt younger and sprier when in the presence of those of advanced age and infirmity.

Aldo co-piloted the wheelchair bearing his new friend, around the blooming gardens of the Sisters of Mount Carmel nursing home.

"You know, my mind's eye remembers all the beautiful sights that eight-plus decades of springs have given me; so, I don't miss being able to clearly see their wonders, I have committed them to memory," said Tony Assunta to his new friend.

"Ah, but just smell that, eh Assunta?" urged Aldo.

The old man strained forward slightly, raised his chin, and sniffed the air expectantly, as if a connoisseur of fine wine, deep in concentration, detecting each secret nuance of the earth's complex bouquet, "Cat shit!"

"Correct! When the cat shit thaws, you know spring really is here," chuckled Aldo.

"Yes," nodded the partially blind man sagely, "once you can smell the cat shit, there'll be no more frost and the grape vines are safe."

They progressed at a leisurely pace past the formal beds and borders near the entrance to the allée of pleached lilacs which terminated at a small meadow bordering the south bank of the Humber River, whose waters were high and rapid with the season's thaw.

A long-deceased resident, an avid gardener, bequeathed the planting of scores of muscari hyacinth, blue bells, daffodils, and crocus, left to naturalize as they may. The effect was charming, creating a fragrant oasis of quiet contemplation and respite, as much for the staff and residents as for visiting friends and relations.

Aldo and Assunta paused to linger in the warmth

of the late afternoon sun, listening to the urgent rippling and plashing of the river's swift current. Suddenly, a stiff, cool breeze picked-up and the two men, feeling its warning chill, instinctively moved off to the protection of the home.

Aldo returned his friend to the large, pleasant room he shared with Bud Chaplain; a longtime friend of Cheech's who today was feeling too tired to join his 'bunkie' on a spin around the grounds. Cheech had been visiting Bud regularly, ever since a concussive fall, followed by a long stay in rehab, put an end to his living independently. A life-long bachelor, Bud had no wife or children; as a late-octogenarian, he had the misfortune to outlive most of his family and friends.

The broadcast of the college football game Cheech and Bud were watching was over, and dinnertime was drawing near, a repast the two visitors were invited to share, but usually begged-off as the food was cafeteria quality and both men drew the line at sacrificing their stomachs for the sake of friendship. As Cheech rose to say his goodbyes, Aldo reached for his cap, knocking-over a framed photograph of Assunta and his wife, which judging by their attire, was likely taken on a milestone anniversary.

Stooping to replace it, Aldo noticed a smaller,

tattered photo tucked into the back of the frame, the kind taken by the Kodak box Brownie everyone in the fifties and sixties possessed to capture their family's' lives, whether in defeat or victory over the struggle to happiness. This souvenir spoke of ease and happiness; a day at a lake where a young curvaceous sun-suited blonde, standing at the water's edge, held the hand of a stout, deeply tanned toddler, his damp unruly curls, tumbled over a broad forehead, his heavily lashed, penetrating eyes, stared fearlessly into the camera.

Beside the pair, probably mother and son, stood an older, broadly smiling version of the boy, a barrel-chested, well-muscled man, whose burly arm was draped casually around the shoulders of the laughing blonde.

Aldo regarded the photo bearing the marginal imprint of 1963, and gave a short, low whistle. "Who's this, Assunta, Marilyn Monroe?"

"What? Oh, you must be looking at the little picture of my cousin's wife and her boy, yep, she was a real 'looker', a figure, as you say, like Marilyn, a smile like hers too." Assunta grinned winsomely at the memory.

"Is that you beside her?" Aldo asked.

"Yeah, that's me, the second time I came to Canada. My cousin and I rented a cottage at Wasaga

Beach that summer."

"Oh, the cousin must be taking the picture, eh? The boy, he favors your side, is built like you," Aldo observed looking from the photo to his friend.

"Yes, I guess so. He looks a little like my side, stocky and dark."

Aldo set the picture down carefully in an angled placement between two other images of long-gone relatives in high collars, bustled skirts, and stiff corsets.

"What did you do when you first came here, Assunta?" asked Aldo.

"Pretty much the same as the second time; I studied to get my realtor's license and moonlighted playing accordion in an Italian band doing dances, weddings etc., we were very popular, and the money was pretty good."

"So, what happened, why did you go back?" asked Aldo.

"Oh, you know, family obligations, my dad, a widower wasn't well, my only sibling, a brother had moved to Rome, so I came back to manage dad's business affairs. After he died, I returned to Toronto with my inheritance and became a partner in my cousin's real estate brokerage."

"Didn't you find it hard to get into business when you first came over?" said Aldo.

"Not really, I could read and write English fairly well, once I was here, speaking it came easy. Anyway, we usually spoke Italian within the band and in real estate we dealt mainly with Italians then. You know the economy during the fifties and sixties was good for us, there were lots of jobs, many unionized and the building trades boomed."

"Yes, those were the good old days. Not like now, it's much harder to get established in this economy, whether you're an immigrant or not," Cheech concluded. They all nodded in agreement, then exchanging thanks and good-byes, the two visitors left.

CHEECH NAVIGATED HIS bulky, four-door Buick down the winding drive of the home, out onto the wide thoroughfare, the volume of its usual weekday traffic reduced to a late Sunday afternoon trickle.

Reaching to turn the volume of the car radio down, Aldo mused, "That Tony Assunta, he's done well for himself, must have a decent stash, eh?"

"Oh yeah, his cousin did very well in that business before he passed away, heart attack at thirty-three," recalled Cheech.

"Son of a bitch," exclaimed Aldo, shaking his

head in disgust.

"Yep, quite a shame for his young wife and kid, but her husband left them well-provided. Anyway, when Tony retired, he sold the brokerage for a pretty penny. I remember Bud telling me that him and his wife Cora travelled a good deal, cruises, and such, had a lovely home too. Too bad they never had kids, but on the other hand, they were free to come and go as they pleased, no worries," Cheech sighed, contemplating such a carefree and lucrative lifestyle.

"So, you'd think he'd have a private room in one of those newer fancy 'senior lifestyle' communities," said Aldo.

"Naw, I think he likes the pace and the people there, it's small, peaceful and he and Bud are good company for each other, been friends for years."

"Well, that's good, but I can't imagine having to bunk with *you*, old man!" laughed Aldo.

"What? So, who's inviting you? Anyway, what's wrong with me?"

"Nothing except for having the highest decibel snore known to mankind."

"I don't snore!" retorted Cheech, thumping the steering wheel.

"You do snore, and loudly, it's a good thing your dear departed wife was hard of hearing," Aldo exclaimed.

"Carmela wasn't hard of hearing," Cheech insisted.

"Oh yeah, then why did you always have to repeat yourself to her, Cheech?"

"Ah baloney, she was just hard of listening."

At that they both laughed, remembering Carmela's indifference to heeding anything Cheech said that she didn't want to hear.

LAYING DOWN THE LAW

JESSE BUSIED HERSELF, impatiently rummaging through the cupboards of her parents' kitchen, noisily opening, and closing drawers, a subterfuge while waiting for her signal.

Meanwhile, down the hall, her grandfather, still in bathrobe and slippers whispered huskily into his blue tooth, opening his door a crack to squint at the distracted figure of son-in-law Nick, who was performing his usual disorganized ritual of searching the wrong pockets for his keys, cleansing their contents of obsolete paper, checking his wallet to discover less than he expected, then finally making it past the door into the early light of a cold, March morning.

"Right, right…got it, buddy," Aldo replied, his voice now free to rise with his enthusiasm, "so the odds are good? Thanks Sam, right, my people'll be talking to your people, ha, ha! Jess!" Aldo bellowed, "the coast is clear, we have lift-off."

"Finally! Nonno there's only so many times I can pretend to be interested in dad's spice drawer, 'specially since he knows I can't cook. God, he always takes *sooo* long to leave the house," moaned Nick's exasperated daughter.

"I know. He's worse than any woman."

"Nonno, please don't be so misogynist."

"Don't you mean 'chauvinist'?"

"Oh, never mind. The envelope please," she said, imitating a drum roll as her grandfather slipped their bets and his money in and taped it closed. Snatching it from him, holding it up to the light to see its contents, Jess mugged, "And the winners are?"

"Never you mind, miss sassy, just pony-up your share and we'll be square!" Aldo joked poking her in the ribs as she winced at his corny humor.

"MY share? You should tip me for delivery, nonno. Why you we just bet on the track, instead of this illegal sports gambling, with like uh, 'Nick the Greek', in the Seven-Eleven parking lot?" she challenged her grandfather, not for the first time.

"Like I told you, I like helping-out the local economy."

"You mean *under*ground economy, don't you?" corrected Jesse.

"Whatever, one way or the other, it's all the economy, stupid."

"Oh, wow nonno, you're a regular Bill Clinton." Jesse rolled her eyes.

"Right" he said giving her a peck on the cheek and a nudge on her back. "Now hustle or you'll miss 'the bread man'."

He watched down the hallway after her, urging a hasty retreat, then flopped onto the wing chair in front of the television, tuning into the station listing last night's Lotto winners. He surveyed the TV tray containing a roll of tickets, clicked the cap off his hi-liter and searched the screen for the nocturnal gifts Lady Luck may have bestowed upon him.

"*Porca vacca*! Not one, ach! This Lotto crap's for suckers anyway."

Aldo tore the tickets in half, then reaching for his iPod, a birthday present from Jesse, he thought, *never mind kid, our other bet'll pay off.* And with that he pushed the ear buds in place, reclined his lazy-boy and was transported by the cool magic of Peter Appleyard and Lionel Hampton's jazzy, 1979 vibraphone duet, on *Seven, Come Eleven*.

Where is that little twerp? Jesse said to herself as she stood in the 'usual place' by the side of the Seven-Eleven, staring pointlessly at the driveway entrance as if trying to conjure the metallic blue Trans Am, replete with orange flame decals on the hood and fuzzy dice dangling from the rear-view mirror. The quintessential 'Ginomobile', which came with its own annoying little misogynist driver, who apparently thought that most girls' parents had named them either 'Hey, Baby' or 'Hi, Sexy'. Where were the Kens of her childhood imagining? Barbie's bland, affable consort may not have had a cock, or balls, but she was sure he would have had politically correct manners.

Jesse quickly pushed her sunglasses down from her forehead to cover her eyes as the offensive sight of contact, 'Nick, the Greek', pulled in beside her, his grandiose street name after the American celebrity bookie. She always wore her darkest shades when making a drop, so she could roll her eyes undetected at his inane comments.

"Hi, sexy! Don't you look fine today; all dressed-up for me?"

"Oh, how did you guess? I *so* look forward to

these tedious little encounters," Jesse mocked, leaning over to pass the envelope containing her and nonno's weekly sports' bet, teasing him with a provocative flash of her ample cleavage. Paradoxically, this exchange always made her feel nasty and sexy, fantasizing playing a streetwalker paying her vile pimp. The thought made her shudder at once with revulsion and sexual thrill.

"Well, now," he said fingering the envelope, "that's a nice little bundle; speaking of nice little bundles sexy, care to go for a spin?"

Jesse snorted with derision; judging by his pimply complexion and lack of self-assurance, barely disguised by the ludicrously brash come-on's, she guessed the kid to be about seventeen, "Oh little boy, don't you think I'm too mature for you?" she cooed.

"Huh, I thought you were going to say, too fat, but that's okay I like women with big butts!" he sneered back.

"Keep talking like that kid and your little gonads'll be keeping your tonsils company." Jesse's parting invective was barely out of her mouth, when a police car pulled-up behind the Trans Am effectively blocking it in, while Jesse heard a voice immediately behind her ordering her to stay where she was. Frozen in disbelief, as the female officer pulled both Jesse's hands behind her back, she stiffened, suddenly feeling the cold steel of handcuffs around her wrists.

AFTER SHOWING THE detectives out and quietly shutting the front door, Nick coolly and decisively turned both locks, the click of the deadbolts sliding into place audible in the tense stillness of the adjacent living room. The authority of the gesture resonated with the solemn gathering of his family who sat alert and rigid with anticipation.

Standing inside the doorway, arms folded across his expansive chest, Nick addressed his father-in-law, who stared straight ahead through angry eyes.

"Who the hell do you think you are, eh? Nathan Detroit or is it Lucky Luciano? Well, like him, your luck has just run out."

"I can't believe you've betrayed our trust and done something as risky as this!" joined Lidia, rising to face her father.

Aldo tightly grasped both arms of the wing chair and jutted-out his chin.

"Oh, come down off your high horses why don't you; it's only a little sports' betting, not the white slave trade…for chrissake!" Looking from his infuriated daughter to his stolid son-in-law, Aldo continued, "Huh, and don't act as though you've never done anything illegal." He wagged an accusing finger.

"No!" Lidia and Nick shot back in unison.

"Oh yeah?" Aldo started, quickly glancing sideways at a timorous Jesse and curling his lips, "Then I guess that wasn't marijuana you were smoking during your late-night giggle-fests, the ones you held while you thought your baby daughter and I were fast asleep. The only diff is you weren't busted!" Feeling triumphant, Aldo had turned the tables.

"Mom! Dad?" An incredulous Jesse looked to her parents.

"Oh, just shut-up!" shrieked Lidia, stomping her foot in exasperation at her father's betrayal.

Nick moved towards his wife and placed a hand on her shoulder, a gesture meant to regain her composure, as he regained control of the issue.

"No, we weren't, but you and *my daughter* were, and now you'll have to face a court and give testimony – be a stoolie, just to keep the Crown from pressing charges; how will your backroom buddies like that, do you think?" Nick chided.

Aldo sank back against the chair and looked down at his folded hands.

Lidia stood beside her husband and shook her head, "Never mind acting aggrieved, dad…there'll be no more gambling of *any* kind while you're living in this house. End of discussion," she said, planting her hands on her hips.

Suddenly propelled by furious indignation, Aldo sprang to his feet muttering angrily, stomped-off down the hall to his room. He back-kicked the door shut, fell into his lazy-boy, held his head in his hands and silently cursed.

Nick sighed and looked to Lidia with chagrin, "Please tell me he didn't just say, 'You're not the boss of me'."

Jesse took this opportunity to try sliding past her parents, slinking down the hallway to her basement suite, where she planned to lay low for the next few days, a plan quickly foiled by her mother's sudden grip around her upper arm, "Oh no, you don't!"

"What?" Jesse feigned innocence.

"Sit down," commanded Nick, barely containing his fury. She did as she was told, shrinking herself into a tiny, pitiable form as a defense against the indignant rebuke she knew was coming.

"Do you ever think about the consequences your actions have on the rest of the family, like me, for example? I'm a professor! Thank god, one with tenure – *for now*. How do you think this would look to the president, the governors and to my students, if you were to be charged; it would be reported, gleefully and salaciously in the papers. How am I to have any credibility with the parents whose offspring are in my care, or have any moral authority with the students themselves?" Nick bellowed.

"I can't believe you're invoking the outrage of the parents and 'your moral authority' as a professor, dad you teach *Art*, not religion! What's next, 'What will the neighbors think?' Puhleeze!" Jesse sighed, impatiently jiggling her foot.

"You may not yet understand the realities of building a professional career, seeing as you don't even have a damn job, but your reputation and the actions of my family, especially while under my roof, reflects on *me*!" her father insisted.

Scowling, Jesse contemplated the carpet; refusing to acknowledge Nick's point, when Lidia picked-up the theme of collateral damage.

"You can avert your eyes all you want to lady, but you can't escape the implications of your greed on both our reputations; I work for a magazine, one which I am sure would not be best pleased to see your criminal actions disseminated on social media, whilst the mother of said miscreant gives guidance to society on the rules of courtesy and civility. Which apparently do not extend to abiding by its laws; thanks, a lot!"

"Is that it?" Jesse said quietly.

"Yes, for now," replied Nick, whose fury, Jesse knew, was finally spent and there would be little of it by tomorrow, except for a certain quiet chill. Jesse rose, arms still folded defensively across her chest, she angled past her unmoved and unmoving mother, whose searing glare she felt even though her head remained resolutely inclined.

"Well, that's the end of our daughter's innocence," Nick said, unhappily.

"And her self-righteousness," added Lidia, brightening.

THREE DAYS LATER, Jesse rotated the knob of her grandfather's door, opened it slightly, then pressing a cheek against it, whispered through the crack, "Nonno, can I come in?"

"Sure, sure, come…sit down," Aldo gestured, straining to make eye contact with Jesse over the back of his reclined lazy-boy. He turned-off The Wheel of Fortune, he was only half-watching, returned his chair to the upright position and gave his granddaughter his full attention. She sank with a whoosh into the familiar comfort of her old orange, suede beanbag chair. When her nonno moved-in, she dragged it from the attic to his ground floor quarters so they could watch TV together, play backgammon and have cozy chats.

"I was just thinking about you," he started, "and that I owe you an apology."

"For what, nonno?" Jesse asked.

Leaning forward to meet her gaze, Aldo half-whispered, "Jess, I never should've encouraged you to gamble, illegally or otherwise…I'm sorry, I caused trouble for you, and set a bad example."

"Oh, nonno," she said dismissively, "it's not like I'm ten years old, I knew what I was doing and only did it for the extra money and to help you out; I'm not addicted or anything. Anyway, in the end they didn't even charge me, you're the one who's in trouble," Jesse said, her voice rising.

"I know, but don't worry, I got that covered." Winking, he made a sideways motion with his hand as if to brush crumbs from a table. "…And don't ask".

"Okay I won't, but tell me this, why do you gamble? You don't need the money…or do you?" Jesse said, narrowing her eyes.

"No, no, I'm fine!" he insisted loudly.

Sitting back in his chair, resting his cheek on his fist for a moment, he contemplated the answer, "I guess it's for the challenge, to beat the odds, to be able to sit back after my team wins and feel like I accomplished something. Getting my just reward for being smarter than the rest, getting one over on the boss.

"You know Jess, it's hard for the 'average Joe' to feel special in this world, to be a hero. And maybe I wanted to be a hero, to show you how smart your nonno is instead of the jackass that I really am." He averted his eyes, ashamed to meet hers.

Jesse was taken aback by this admission; she always saw her nonno as smart, tough, and self-assured. It surprised her that he sought her approval and admiration. Not that he and she hadn't always been close friends and confederates, it's just that she never saw him in a humble attitude, and it saddened her, he suddenly seemed defeated.

Struggling to free herself from her childhood chair, she leant over to kiss her beloved grandfather's cheek, then quietly left the room.

Chapter Three

SUMMER

"Aren't you worried, Nick?" Lidia asked, sliding file folders, day timer and tablet into her hand-stitched, red nubuck leather valise, a present from Nick on their last trip to Venice. Nick was engrossed in lavishly spreading the last of the homemade raspberry jam on his second warm, buttered crumpet, this being one of the mornings when he didn't have a class until eleven-thirty.

"Oh, a bit, but Aldo was adamant that we let him face the music alone, in his own way and we have to respect that. Anyway, he's probably very embarrassed."

"Dad, embarrassed? You must be kidding, beneath his thin veneer of bravado and bluster, lies more bravado and bluster. Still, I'm afraid he's going to dig himself in deeper, lose his temper and be charged with contempt of court," she grimaced, checking her watch.

"Nah, he's not that stupid and anyway, he won't

be entirely alone," Nick said through a sly smile.

"Go on professor, you interest me strangely," said Lidia leaning on the island counter, resting her chin on her fist.

"Well," Nick replied, brushing a few errant crumbs from his shirt, "he specified that *we* shouldn't be there, he never said anything about Frank not going, now did he?"

"Nick, you are a lovely, wicked genius," Lidia smiled as she put her arms around her husband's neck and gave him a loud kiss.

"Well, I can't deny it," he sighed, very pleased with himself.

"Full report then, before he gets home?" Lidia said, grabbing her valise, leaving hastily for work.

WITNESS FOR THE PROSECUTION

LATER THAT AFTERNOON, Nick sat in the darts' room of the rambling Victorian house, raised his perfectly poured Guinness from the slightly sticky coaster and drank appreciatively.

The pub had been converted from a domestic to a commercial purpose, like many other late nineteenth-century, rambling old red brick monsters of

Toronto's gentrified Annex area. This particularly capacious and fussily gabled Queen Anne was now a pub/restaurant divided into several themed rooms and a summer patio which proved a goldmine to its owners, being within walking distance to the university and its perpetually thirsty denizens.

In truth though, Nick preferred to do his imbibing further afield where he was unlikely to encounter or be served by one of his disgruntled students. Nevertheless, today the venue proved convenient for him and Frank, who had only forty minutes to spare between courtroom espionage duty and teaching his Religious Education class.

"Where's mine? I could murder a cold lager; it must be thirty-six degrees in the shade. It's a sauna out there. God, I hate this city in the summer, it's insufferable, but here we are for our sins, both teaching summer courses to the desperate and aggrieved," complained Father Frank, grimacing at his companion as he lowered his damp and disheveled self onto the banquette, his battered briefcase installed beside him.

As Nick hailed a waiter, Frank launched into an animated account of the court's proceedings and Aldo's 'performance' as a Crown witness.

"You know Nick, your father-in-law missed his true calling, he's an incredible actor, somewhat of the silent screen era though, more Charlie Chaplin than Charlie Sheen."

"Oh, how's that?" queried Nick, raising his eyebrows in surprise.

"From his wheelchair, it seems he has difficulty speaking 'broken English' intelligibly through his ill-fitting, clicking dentures, which is moot, as despite having stereo hearing aids, which he fiddles with constantly, he cannot clearly hear the questions put to him. Then there's his tragic visual disability he bravely bears through the thick glasses it is his cross to bear!" exclaimed Frank, continuing with his narrative, "So brave, so stalwart was he in the face of such cruel adversities old age and infirmity present, one wonders if beatification upon his demise might not be out of reach. I'll put in a good word with the bishop, you never know your chances, seems that John Paul II was on a holy tear, seeding the hagiography with celestial supporters."

"Ha, ha!" Nick threw back his head in robust laughter, slamming his open palm down on the table, nearly spilling their drinks, "The old devil."

"Who? Aldo or Pope John Paul?" chuckled Frank as he raised a well-earned pint to his smiling lips.

"So, was he dismissed?" asked Nick, waiting for an answer while his companion swallowed a deep gulp of lager.

"Entirely and with exasperation," beamed Father Frank.

DIM SUM DRAMA

JESSE AND HER friends were bunched-up around the small Formica table, sharing dim sum from a heavily laden lazy-Susan. They had just been to the Art Gallery of Ontario, where they attended an exhibition of erotic fin-de-siècle Dada and Impressionist photography curated by one of their professors, Annie Prentiss, lecturer in the course, Feminist Revisionist Art History, and the Male Gaze.

The Chinese restaurant was one of their favorite haunts as it was old school mom and pop, homey, inexpensive, unpretentious. The proprietors were as quirky as their iconic sign, an old neon which once displayed the simple boast, Good Food. 'Good', arranged vertically, and 'Food', spelled horizontally, their terminal 'd's' had long been extinguished and never replaced, giving the establishment its neighborhood nickname, The Goo-Foo.

Amongst the laughing, chopstick brandishing group, was Tully Cooper, a lively, flame-haired, natural comedian who sometimes did short stand-up gigs in local bars opening for her boyfriend's funk/soul group, The Last Band. This afternoon she was in fine form, effusive and flushed from her third Tsing Tsao, "Wow! Did you see the bushes on those models?" she exclaimed a little too loudly.

"Uh-huh, definitely no waxing or bling south of the border those days," laughed Athina, nudging Jesse who sat, a little uncomfortably, beside her.

"Yeah, Brazilian, Vajazzle, that's *sooo 2001*! What we like is the Big Bush, the Fluffy Muffy, the Furry Ferret and the deluxe... Full-length Mink! That's right girls, a bush so beauteous it curls out waaay beyond the bikini line, you know everyone will be rocking that look this summer, SO START GROWING YOURS NOW!" Tully had them in stitches.

Then Kate, suddenly feeling brazen offered, "What a great idea for a 'personal care' boutique franchise, call it The Snatch Hatch, with style options like, Rasta Dreads, dies like the Candy Floss, or the ultimate for back-to-earth green gals...The Chia Pet!" She leant back gratified by the steady crescendo of hysterical laughter and having gone Tully one better.

Soon after the women exhausted their bawdy banter, food and drink, Kate, and Tully settled their tabs, and headed off to Black Jack's, Tully's brother's place, as Kate wanted to buy a set of new 'discounted' headphones for her brother's birthday.

Black Jack was a bitter twenty-seven year old software engineer whose decently paid and highly trained position had been 'Bengalied'; out-sourced to India at half his former wage, and finding it hard to make ends meet doing retail jobs in one of North America's most expensive cities, turned to selling pirated software, pirated computer games, various other dubious electronics and potent home-grown 'artisan' weed and hashish.

He was in the process of enjoying a joint, when a few sharp raps on his front door dispelled his foggy reverie; Black Jack peered out the spy-hole to see the familiar faces of his sister and her somewhat solvent friend, or as he liked to think of them: dinner.

BACK AT THE now silent and nearly deserted restaurant, Jesse and Athina sat quietly alone amongst the detritus left from lunch; the greasy plates stained with ponzu sauce, piles of broken chopsticks, crumpled paper napkins, empty beer bottles and a scattering of unopened fortune cookies. Athina broke the awkward silence, "Thanks for staying, Jess. I really need to talk to you."

Jesse did not meet Athina's eyes, just shrugged

her shoulders, in a gesture of indifference,

"S'okay. I guess you want to patch things up, now Ainsworth's moving to Montreal."

"That's partly it, I think we could and should be friends again. Jess, I really miss you. You and I have been like sisters since kindergarten, and I hate what's happened to our relationship."

"Well," said Jess looking up at her friend, "we know who's to blame for that, now don't we."

"Yes, okay, I'm sorry about Ainsworth, I really regret how that happened. I didn't know you were still hung-up on him, so torn up about it. You didn't say."

"Because I didn't blab about my hurt feelings, which were more like wounded pride, I guess, doesn't mean it's okay that you move in on him, start sleeping with him…after all we'd *just* broken-up!" Jesse's face was flushed with resentment.

"Jess, you have every right to be mad at me, but can't you forgive me too?" Athina implored, reaching out for her hand.

After an uncomfortable pause, Jesse said, "Maybe I can forgive you; I've really missed you," she conceded, giving her errant friend a half-smile.

"Thanks Jess, I'd hate to lose my best friend and only sister!"

Their make-up drama safely over, the tension

between both girls slackened as they sat back feeling relaxed, falling into the familiar pattern of their intimate exchanges. Athina tossed Jesse a fortune cookie, "Well, let's see what the Oriental oracle has for us today. You First, Jess."

Jesse snapped the cookie in half, teased out the slim length of paper. Squinting at the small, blurry print, she read, "'People admire your assertiveness'," then tossed it aside. "Huh, hardly the oracle of Delphi. Now you."

"'It is easier to resist at the beginning than it is at the end', well, it's nothing if not cryptic. Hey, let's both buy lottery tickets for tonight's draw with the fortune cookies' lucky numbers."

"Okay, we each get a share in each other's fortunes, deal?" Jesse put out her hand.

"Deal!" Athina shook on it.

They both sat back, not yet ready to part company, when Jesse ventured, "Hey, have you met Tully's new boyfriend, Dave?"

"Uh-huh," Athina nodded.

"Well, what do we think...cute?"

"No. Way too much ink for my taste," Athina said, referring to the vivid tattoos covering both arms and one side of Dave's neck.

"You know he's got a cobra in his pants," whispered Jesse.

"What? How do *you* know?"

"He only showed me the head!" laughed Jesse.

"The head? Of what?" Athina raised her voice.

"Of the cobra, it's drawn around the opening of his navel like a mouth."

"Gawd," Athina exclaimed. "How sad will that look when he's sixty-five and his 'six-pack' is a blobby beer belly?"

They both snickered at the thought. As Jesse ordered them a fresh pot of chai, Athina kept the conversation in neutral territory, reluctant to address the explosive issue, which was her real purpose. She rattled-on instead with more innocuous 'girlie gossip', so it felt as if the congeniality between them had never been breached.

Jesse hardly listened to Athina's breezy chatter, focusing instead on her companion's expressive, smoky-grey eyes rimmed by a fringe of long black lashes, the envy of all their friends from grade school on. Her wide mouth and gently curved lips were slender and tinted with a flush of peach, the rest of her smooth complexion, a delicate ivory.

Yes, thought Jesse, Athina was certainly a classic natural beauty who was aptly named. And as she poured her a second cup of hot tea, she realized just how much she had missed her beautiful best friend.

There was a momentary silence while Athina

alternately cooled, then sipped the steaming beverage. A silence which Jess, dying to broach the Ainsworth issue filled, "So, I guess Ainsworth's film grant finally came through…when does he start production in Montreal?"

"Oh, in about two weeks," said Athina, who knew the inevitable was now unavoidable.

"I guess we'll both be glad to see him go," Jesse sighed with certainty.

"Well, not exactly both of us, Jess… I'll be going with him."

Jesse found it took all her willpower to stop from jumping-up and screaming, opting instead for a grimace of disbelief and a shrill challenge, "What are you thinking? What about graduation? You'll miss the exams! You're throwing everything away!"

At that, Athina's contrition towards her long-term friend dissolved and her inner resolve rose to meet the occasion, "Oh please, that piece of paper is more for our parents' benefit than ours. It's just an insurance, something to fall back-on, and like Ainsworth says, if you spend your life securing things to fall back-on, that's just what you'll do – fall back!"

"Yeah right, he *would* say that because he just wants you there as someone *he* can fall back-on, ever considered that, huh? Ainsworth's a selfish, insecure man, who's just using you."

Jesse's blunt flash of insight stunned Athina as much as Jesse herself, who bolted from the table feeling an uneasy rush of triumph. Athina, still seated, tried to recover her composure and dignity by making an elaborate pretense of ease and contemplation before the hovering busboy; casually sipping the last of her tea, carefully counting-out the money for the bill, and inwardly praying to make it home before she broke down in tears.

JOLLY JOSH

BACK AT HOME, Jesse's surge of triumph crashed into remorse as she lay on her bed, admonishing herself for her outburst. *Well idiot, that didn't go too well, now did it...maybe it's for the best though, I need some distance from all of this.*

Jesse had long been aware that she harbored a girl crush on Athina ever since grade three and time had not extinguished it. Quite the contrary, as time passed and the trajectory of their lives coalesced, Jesse's feelings for Athina had grown as had her subtle jealousy of the ever-widening circle of friends Athina attracted.

Was this just a 'girl-crush', attributable as much to their simpatico creative spirits as it was to their 'only daughter' condition? Jesse was perplexed by her feelings, but one thing she understood, Athina did not share them. In fact, Athina had a lively, casual generosity of spirit, which she bestowed upon diverse friends, making her interesting and popular. Jesse, on the other hand, was possessive and slightly wary of her fellow beings. She was not very gregarious, but a stalwart, canny, and practical friend.

Lately, Jesse had become worried over her emotional and social dependence upon the attractive Athina...making her wonder, was her 'gal-crush' 'normal'? And what was 'normal' anyway? So far, it had only been Athina who roused these feelings in her and even though, to her mother's despair, she was never a 'girlie girl', she still cared if she was attractive to men.

She recalled the time when in grade six, she and Athina, fantasizing about Johnny Depp, practiced kissing him, first on the fleshy folds of the inside of their fists, then at Jesse's suggestion, on each other's lips, sweetly, sloppily, briefly.

Jesse found that, like Katy Perry, she kissed a girl, and she liked it. Athina, unmoved, laughed it off, jumping-up to show off, crossing her arms across her chest, then wrapping them around her back;

facing the mirror she emulated her lover's amorous embraces, miming Johnny Depp feeling her up. They both broke-up laughing, rolling off Jesse's bed, onto the pink shag carpet.

Jesse laughed out loud at the memory and with the Katy Perry song still playing in her head, she decided to watch the video of, *I Kissed a Girl and I Liked It,* on YouTube. Just after logging-in, a pop-up box notified her of an email from Josh, a nice, fun guy with whom she had shared a beer, a joint, then a long, wet kiss in the back of a cab on the way home from a group show.

"Yes!" she responded to his invite to the Horseshoe Tavern to hear his friend's band. Jolly Josh… tall, dark and handsome, with sleepy, deep-brown eyes. Easy-going Josh, a good kisser, was perhaps exactly what she needed right now. She just wished he'd ditch that stupid man-bun.

HODGE PODGE

AT THE HEAD of *Your Best Life's* conference table, erect and unflagging, sat Editor in Chief, Ms. Hilda Braun, who peered imperiously over her glasses, down a prominent equine nose, at her editorial staff.

They were exhibiting various signs of Friday afternoon meeting fatigue; fidgeting in swivel chairs, politely coughing into expensive wrist watches, tugging at the edges of hems, twisting grimy French cuffs, and tapping gnawed fingernails on silenced iPhones as they would have on cigarette packages in a by-gone era.

"Well, I think that's all for now. You've made *some* decent progress this month in restructuring content-focus to align with the new marketing plan, but you will, holidays or no, produce more and better soon, I'm sure," she pronounced.

Hilda Braun's unremarkable name evolved, as her remarkable rise in corporate status, to 'Brunhilde', a nickname her aggrieved staff would insist, behind her back, was entirely justified. Now, having sucked most of the oxygen from the room and the hope for a relaxing holiday, with her terse commendation cloaking a benign reprimand, she rose and left the conference room dogged by her faithful P.A., Clive Snodden.

"Well!" ...

"Don't say it," warned Lidia, raising a stern index finger to the lips of her indignant colleague, Shelton.

"Oh, alrighty then Miss Mew, what do you, our exalted editor have to say about Brunhilde's damnation by faint praise, and her imposition on our well-earned summer holidays? I mean if I had wanted to work for God Almighty, I would've joined the church," Shelton hissed.

A distraught Lidia looked past Shelton's indignant scowl as if a diplomatic answer could be found floating as an apparition behind him, that unfortunately failed to emerge.

"Well, I uh…oh dammit Shelton! You know very well what I'd like to say, but I can't. So… I don't know, just 'suck it up'… won't you, *please*?" She found herself imploring, searching his periwinkle blue eyes for a sign of humor and assent.

"Only for you Miss Mew, and only for now, until the editorial revamp is complete," Shelton promised with a heavy sigh, invoking his pet-name for Lidia, one he adopted, on account of her feline mystique, when she was a charming newbie, sheltered beneath his avuncular wing.

"Thanks for not stirring the pot Shelton, I won't forget this," promised a relieved Lidia.

"Oh, don't worry; you won't get the chance to, because next holiday weekend we're going on an investigative sojourn, down the long and winding roads through Nova Scotia's wine country."

"They have wine in Nova Scotia?" Lidia said raising an eyebrow.

"*They* seem to think so," Shelton responded dryly.

"And food… will there be food?"

"Last time I checked," said Shelton.

"You know what I mean by food Shelton, the kind of comestibles I…we, would eat."

"Look girl, they'll feed you up right. Cods' cheeks, snapped mackerel, Solomon Gundy, hodge podge…the works! It'll be some good," he drawled.

"Shelton, why are you talking like that and what the hell is 'hodge podge'?"

"It's delicious, you'll see, oh and just wait until you discover what part of Solomon is his Gundy!" Shelton rubbed his hands in mock glee. At this, Lidia worried about the depth of the debt Shelton might assume she owed.

Just then, they spied Brunhilde herself leaving the lady's room. She acknowledged their presence with a curt nod of the head and a tight, terse smile, turning her back to them, drawing a drink of water from the cooler. Shelton raised a fist to his mouth and could barely suppress a titter, Lidia's eyes widened, and her face turned ashen.

"Oh, my god," she whispered, "she's tucked the back of her skirt into her panty hose! I'll have to tell her."

Shelton stepped in front of Lidia, barring her way as she tried to make off in the direction of their nemesis, "Oh no you don't. This is the best fun I've had since she swooped in on us; I just knew she wore granny pants."

"Oh, really Shelton, don't be such a brat," Lidia admonished, staring him down.

"Honestly, Miss Mew, I find your lack of commitment to your education in evil, quite disturbing."

"No, Shelton, it's just too mean to let her walk around like that. I'm telling her now."

He watched with chagrin as his acolyte strode past him; then muttered bitterly to himself, *Why does Satan always get the best students?*

BURGUNDY AND BARBEQUE

NICK STOOD IN his baggy cargo shorts and faded rugby shirt, inhaling the fragrance from the glowing embers of the wood burning barbeque. Happily clacking his tongs as he turned over the meats in the mixed-grill supper, he thought, *what a perfect way to celebrate the summer solstice.* Taking a long pull from his frosted beer glass, "Ahhh," he exhaled with deep satisfaction into the clear blue, late afternoon sky.

But his perfect blue-sky moment was soon shattered by an impatient Lidia, engaged in a profane struggle with their recalcitrant garden gate.

"Does madam require assistance?" Nick asked in his best 'Jeeves' imitation.

"Stop being such a smug idiot, and open this frigging gate!" she demanded, rattling the offending barrier.

"At once madam." And with an easy flourish and a barely audible chuckle, Nick released the gate hook from its misaligned, rusty latch, letting his exasperated wife into the garden.

He relieved her of the two bottles of Bichot pinot noir she picked-up on her way home from work. Nick got the garden hose, discharged some cold water into the galvanized bucket waiting for the purpose, and put the bottles of red Burgundy in to chill.

He loved this pinot noir; it was a perfect summer red to serve with a mixed grill. Refreshing, unlike full-bodied tannic reds, quaffing well served at a cool cellar temperature, having a pleasing balance between soft astringency and ripe fruit, it well-complemented barbequed meats.

Meanwhile, Lidia returned to the garden, after spritzing her freshly cleansed face with rose water, donning flip-flops, and an aquamarine tank dress, her long, damp hair secured with a plastic clip. She pulled her chair up to the patio table, beneath the welcome shade of the large market umbrella.

"Uh…finally," she sighed, leaning her head back against the chair's deep, tufted cushion. Then pensive, after a moment, she declared, "Nick, I do believe our house is possessed by a mischievous poltergeist."

"A poltergeist, eh? And what makes you think so?"

"Well, why is it that the stairs, doors, gates and even sometimes windows, inexplicably resist my efforts to open, surmount, slide and otherwise use them as passage to the comfort of my hearth, and the bosom of my loving family?"

She directed this challenge at her skeptical husband who was energetically slathering a lemon and coriander marinade over the spatch-cocked quails.

"You climb into the house through the windows? Why? Aren't the doors enough of a challenge for you?" Nick asked, turning to address his wife.

"Exactly! Even the doors are a challenge, don't you remember when we first moved here, and I was pregnant? You were away at classes and I could not for the life of me open the front door with the new key you had cut, so I went round to the back porch and tried to get in through the kitchen window."

"It's all coming back to me now – the neighbors called the cops as all they could see was your dear little behind as you tried to wriggle your way in," he smiled fondly imagining the scene.

"So embarrassing, the young officer, who looked to be all of nineteen, didn't know whether he should pull me out of the window or push me in. In the end he decided, against my protests, to pull me out. After he saw I was pregnant and I explained myself, he tried the key on the front door and it opened easily. He thought I was mad!" Lidia said, glowering at the memory.

"Astute diagnosis, I'd say," laughed Nick.

"You know there are documented cases of actual poltergeist possession in homes," Lidia asserted.

"You mean, like in the film, *The Amityville Horror*?"

"That was based on a true story, wasn't it?"

"C'mon Lidia, if you have to go to Hollywood for your evidence, then it's pretty thin. Anyway, I don't believe in spooks."

"Oh Nick, course you do. I mean *we* do, we're Roman Catholics, for god's sake, of course we believe in spooks. Remember the Apostles' Creed, "I believe in the Holy Spook, uh, Ghost", now you've got me saying it," Lidia laughed.

"Well," rejoined Nick, "I'm a small 'c' catholic, a kind of reform catholic, like our Jewish friends. Some consider themselves 'cultural Jews' – they put pork on their forks, marry gentiles and erect Christmas trees beside their menorahs, so why not me?"

"You did marry a gentile, stupid," countered Lidia.

"You know what I mean, if the Jews can change their practices and still remain Jews, so why, to be regarded as Catholic, do I have to believe in holy spooks, exorcism, or even the Communion of Saints or as I call them, The Confraternity of Benevolent Lunatics?" Nick countered defiantly.

"Well, now you just sound like a Unitarian," Lidia scoffed. "Anyway, you can't even get yourself to Mass on Sundays. When's the last time we were in church together? Weddings, baptisms and funerals excluded." She wagged her finger at him as he prodded his imagination for an answer less damming than the truth.

"I'll be in church next weekend," he announced brightly.

"Doesn't count, you'll be working, it's your job to shepherd heathen students around the sacred monuments of old Quebec City."

"Just because it's a field trip, doesn't mean it won't have a spiritual dimension," Nick exclaimed loudly, defending his position.

"Yes, I'm sure your fervent prayers will go something like, "Please God, get me out of here and tucked into a nice hot gooey pile of poutine and a cold lager," Lidia sat back in her chair waiting for her husband's riposte.

"O ye of little faith, I am a deeply spiritual person, I just don't need to make a display of my devotion, unlike some," he sniffed.

Deciding to let the matter drop, Lidia made for the wine bucket, removed a chilled bottle, and opened it at the table.

"Pour it out cara, then let it breathe for a bit," Nick advised.

"I will, on the next pour, for now a little swish to aerate will have to do." Lidia took a hearty gulp, pronouncing it excellent.

"Well, I'm very glad your colleague, Shelton, isn't here to witness your sacrilege."

"Shelton's a wine expert Nick, not a wine snob."

"Same dif," Nick shrugged.

"Anyway, as it happens, he's given me the opportunity of further instruction next weekend."

"Oh?" Nick said as he poured himself a glass.

"Yes, he's doing a feature on Nova Scotia's wine and food scene and needs me to accompany him as photographer and dining companion, because Siobhan, our food columnist's got a wedding."

"They have wine in Nova Scotia?" Nick looked surprised.

"Of course, they do, and why not?" Lidia said, as if the matter was obvious.

"Dunno, just something about 'New Scotland' that doesn't immediately bring wine chateaus and vineyards to mind…anyway, why isn't he taking a staff photographer?"

"Because the few remaining, who haven't been felled by Brunhilde's austerity hatchet, are on assignment to other photo shoots. And I am trained you know, in the pre-digital days when we had darkrooms and celluloid film.

"Now, anyone with a rudimentary understanding of lighting and composition can take a pretty good photograph. You don't need Karsh to take a few sexy stills of wine bottles and lobsters," Lidia said peevishly.

"I remember when we first met in Rome, you were doing some freelance photography on the side. Every weekend, I followed you all over the seven hills of that 'infernal' city, capturing the vanishing, idyllic country life," Nick recalled.

"That was fun, wasn't it? You were very chivalrous, shouldering all my equipment, helping me set-up in whatever awkward venue, in whichever obscure hill town I found picturesque."

"Huh, they were all picturesque, but nothing as picturesque as you in those tight capris, saucy kitten heels and perky pony-tail. All that astride a red Vespa, revving the engine and honking the horn when you picked me up. Made me weak at the knees," Nick said, closing his eyes.

"Oh, and all along I thought it was just the art. Didn't you think you'd discovered an early Michelangelo? As I recall it was a Madonna lactans, a nursing Madonna, right?"

"Yes, a lovely bas relief tondo of a young Madonna nursing Jesus on the temple steps. But alas, not a Michelangelo, just the work of an obscure, adept student," Nick sighed.

Then returning to the present, he declared, "Well anyway, I guess that's both of us sorted for the long weekend?"

"Yes, no rest for the wicked," Lidia said, as she dressed and tossed the salad, while Nick brought his platter of perfectly browned, succulent meats to the table.

Lidia passed a salad-laden plate to Nick, then helped herself to a chunk of fennel sausage, some quail, and a petite medallion of spring lamb, "Mmm, oh Nick, this smells so good!" she said, smiling at her happy, relaxed husband.

By midnight, there was a cool breeze luffing the sheers on the Ponti's bedroom window; a full moon beamed through the translucent fabric, casting an amber glow over the bed and the naked figures, languidly entwined upon it.

"I'm so sorry, cara," Nick said tenderly, combing his fingers through her tousled hair.

"Oh, don't say that it's lovely just being together, my head on your chest, listening to your heartbeat," she ran her index finger along the cleft between his collar bones, down along the soft curling furrow of hair leading to his navel.

"Just the same, it's been a while; don't think I'm not aware of it and how you probably feel."

"I feel content; don't worry about me. I think you need to focus on your health right now. I know it's normal at a certain age to sometimes have difficulty keeping an erection, but you're right, it's been a while since we fully made love. Really Nick, only a doctor can determine if this is just age-related, a simple test, that's all you need."

"A simple test, eh?" Nick sat up and swung his legs over the side of the bed. "I hate the idea of it." With that, he pushed himself to his feet and made for their bathroom.

Lidia lay on her side, her head resting on her raised forearm, her free hand gathering the sheets up over her naked hips and belly.

"I know Nick, but it has to be done." Then noting that this was his second trip to the bathroom in the last hour, she added, "So, will you make yourself an appointment with Doctor Armstrong?"

Nick grunted something that might be interpreted as assent, but Lidia made a mental note to make the appointment herself first thing Monday morning.

THE NEPTUNE EFFECT

ON THEIR SECOND day in Nova Scotia, Lidia began to unwind, and to her astonishment, really enjoy herself. Once out of Halifax, the previous day's drive across the province to the Minas Basin and the Annapolis Valley with its many charming wineries and farms, was short, just under an hour and without much traffic.

Shelton opened the sunroof on their rental car; the salty air bracing them as they travelled from winery to winery through the verdant countryside, up and over the gently rolling hills following the meandering Avon River. Lidia was entranced.

The atmosphere seemed to work its magic on

Shelton too, his usually cynical attitude and often acerbic humor gave way to an enthusiastic, almost boyish glee. He was dressed in fashionable well-fitting jeans, Top-Sider shoes, a crisp classic, blue-striped Oxford shirt and pale coral cotton pullover.

He looked, Lidia thought, like one of those casual, well-heeled Americans you see in the Ralph Lauren ads or *Land's End* catalogues, ready to board their sailboats for a spin around Hyannis Port or attend a clam bake in Martha's Vineyard. She realized she'd never seen Shelton out of a suit, and quite liked what she saw. Some men just never looked anything but scruffy in casual attire, but her natty companion wore it well.

Today, the itinerary was taking them along the south shore to the historic UNESCO Heritage town of Lunenburg, home of the famous fishing and racing schooner, The Bluenose, fastest clipper ship of the twentieth century and pride of Canadian maritime heritage; Lunenburgers boasting the nickname, 'Bluenosers'.

But before they hit the town, they stopped at a winery specializing in fruit wines and cordials; something neither of them usually drank, but thought interesting to cover nonetheless, this province being known for the quality of its fruits and berries. They sampled a variety of products, which were overall quite palatable, the apple and blueberry wine even delightfully refreshing. Lidia bought a few bottles of elderberry cordial, thinking that Nick could make some culinary use of them in reductions, granitas, and trifles.

Then on to Lunenburg, and its 'painted ladies'; the brightly colored and whimsically gabled eighteenth and nineteenth century wooden houses that boasted the confidence and prosperity of its merchant ships' captains, traders and privateers. Their beacon colors lit-up each side of the steep streets rolling down to the busy harbor, where long ago the men and boys of the town set sail to plunder the bounty of Newfoundland's treacherous Grand Banks, trawl the deep waters of the Bay of Fundy or trade in exotic goods from the Caribbean.

Neptune gave forth his gold, but exacted a terrible tithe, as the widows left behind knew too well. It was for them that the iron lace-cap 'widow's walk' topped the loftiest outlooks; their vigils were not for their men long-lost, but for the scrying moon upon which the faces of those not returning were illuminated, knowledge they were never to utter, their lips screwed down tightly as coffin lids, only their moonstruck eyes might betray its dire portend.

Past these ancient, storied facades, they drove along the shore to the Old Town where Shelton insisted they visit a boutique distillery run from what was once an iron smith's forge. The little distillery produced some very clean, smooth, warming vodkas, a deep luscious amber rum fermented in old French brandy barrels and a lovely cranberry liqueur, made with berries from a local bog; its beautifully clear, vibrant garnet color, and tart, mouthwatering taste made it a perfect gift for the annual 'turkey fests' of Thanksgiving and Christmas. Lidia and Shelton decided to buy a case each and have them shipped back home.

After the late morning's samplings, Lidia found herself in something of a boozy haze, despite Shelton's admonition to, "take it easy," and only try a sip of each offering, her surge of wanton enthusiasm had led her to imprudence, so Tylenol and a stiff espresso at the local coffee roastery was in order. This restorative was just what Lidia needed to head off the thumping headache she sensed was developing.

When they were both refreshed, Shelton stood, returning his wallet to his back pocket, and asked, "Are we ready for a brisk walk-about and then a good gut-bashing lunch?"

"Sure, that's sounds grand, I'd love to get a closer look at the facades of these wonderful historic houses," Lidia said, as Shelton helped her with her chair.

"I think we may do better than that, many of them are inns now, so we can at least get a look in to the front parlors, perhaps some of the unoccupied rooms. There's one place nearby, reputed to have excellent displays of eighteenth-century Delft story tiles surrounding each of its twelve original fireplaces."

"Sounds interesting; I'm familiar with the classic blue and white Delft ceramics, but tell me, what are story tiles?" Lidia asked as they crossed the street in the direction of an imposing dark green, mustard, and maroon three-story bed and breakfast, bearing a heritage plaque dating the building to1787.

"Story tiles are pretty much what they're called, tiles which have a narrative function, often a sequence of images depicting morally instructive tales from Aesop, folklore or the bible."

"You mean something like a comic strip?" asked Lidia.

"Exactly, each tile depicted a scene from the story, remember, not everyone was literate then or could afford books, and tiles were a cheaper commodity. I fancy they would've also been a way to amuse children on long winter nights."

"How interesting, let's get some photos of those. I might use them later," Lidia said, admiring Shelton's erudition. She found his interests and knowledge so diverse, it seemed there was little worthy of interest that he hadn't plumbed the depths of to some degree. Yet, unlike so many erudite people, he did not show-off or pretend to be clever, he simply offered what he knew for what it was worth to anyone who took an interest; he never made his interlocutor feel stupid, although he could easily, given his very sharp wit.

AFTER AN HOURS' ramble through the streets, inns, and antique shops where Lidia bought six vintage tin jelly molds in prettily fluted shapes, they were ready for a prodigious lunch. Lidia was quite surprised at how spoiled for choice they were amongst many good dining establishments, when Shelton decided upon an Italian trattoria that was rumored to have a wine list as sophisticated and expansive as one could find in similar establishments in Toronto. In fact, it had an intimate dining space in the wine cellar called, The Enoteca, being next to where the liquid assets were stored. The stairwell in the one-hundred-sixty-year-old house had been opened-up to be visible from the upper levels, so the cellar was light and airy.

They opted for seating there, where they would have the attention of the resident sommelier with whom Shelton had held a brief interview. Lidia got a few words with the busy chef-owner, and shots of the beautiful old barrels and racks of gleaming, expensive bottles. She was happy that the lighting in The Enoteca was uneven, but atmospheric, giving her pictures a lovely Baroque feeling.

After perusing the lunch menu, Lidia decided on her starter, carciofi alla Giudia, artichokes in the Jewish style, a Roman dish where the artichoke heads are flattened out like sunflowers, then fried until crisp and bronze. Shelton opted for tuna tartar, having the waiter's assurance that the blue fin tuna had come in fresh that day from Prince Edward Island.

Even though artichokes were thought difficult, due to their slight bitterness, to pair with wine, the chef recommended they try a sparkling wine, Nova 7, from Benjamin Bridge. It was a new enterprise by a group of Ontario wine makers who gambled on the fact that this region had a micro-climate and terroir comparable to France's Champagne region. The gamble paid-off well, their first vintage pre-sold, earning enthusiastic reviews.

The reviews were justified, Shelton reckoned, as he thoughtfully sipped the wine, enjoying its clean, crisp minerality and fine effervescence. It put them both in a rather festive mood, the kind for which sparkling wine was created.

After two more courses and equal samplings of wine, Lidia, having this time exercised greater restraint in her consumption, except when it came to their shared dark chocolate torta, was in a dreamy state, completely relaxed and carefree, while Shelton was content and contemplative. "Oh, I think I could quite happily die now, after that perfect meal."

"Well, Miss Mew, don't get too used to it, our culinary adventure tonight is to a 1930's dance and supper club near the motel where we're staying next. The club boasts an 'all you can eat' mussel bar, boiled lobster, and something less than Grade 'AAA' steak, served replete with baked potato in a festive foil jacket, and wine of indeterminate provenance. And put your dancin' shoes on, girl, cause there's' fiddle music too!"

"Oh joy," Lidia responded with no joy whatsoever. "Shelton, can't we just go to a nice beach, walk along the shore, dip our feet in the ocean?"

"Course we can. I have planned for tourist fatigue, just need to get a few splits of that bubbly, then we're on our way to the beach."

THEY BY-PASSED THE new four lane highway to cruise

along the old road which wound its way around the undulating shoreline of Mahone Bay, where past each blind curve there opened-up a scenic vista. The sky was a clear blue, strands of ethereal white clouds streaked across the horizon, the open waters of the bay rippled and sparkled as a procession of silent sailboats glided effortlessly around and between the many small islands within the bay's azure expanse.

Finally, they came to the three iconic old wooden churches, their tall, elegant spires rising to pierce the heavens, releasing the promise of salvation. They left the car to poke around each church and take several pictures. When they had done admiring the architecture, Shelton drove to a mussel and scallop farm on the bay which sold oysters as well. He bought a dozen oysters, they were small and inexpensive, so any they didn't consume could be discarded without remorse.

He concluded their purchase and pulled the door open for Lidia to exit before him, when she hesitated, "Aren't you going to ask where we might find a beach nearby?"

"No need, I know exactly where to go," Shelton smiled enigmatically.

"Well, you must've done a lot of homework planning for this trip," Lidia observed, as she secured her seatbelt and smoothed back her hair.

"Yes, you could say that." Shelton turned the key in the ignition, heading to a pretty sweep of crescent beach, unmarked, and known mainly to locals.

TINY BUBBLES

IT WAS THREE-THIRTY, the grannies were bundling-up their infant charges to head for home, and the preparation of the evening meal. Their vacancy quickly filled with teenagers staking out their territories, planning the late-shift entertainment. Shelton and Lidia ditched their shoes, grabbed the cooler bag, and headed for a promising outcrop of large, flat rocks at the farthest end of the beach from the swarm of teenagers.

Their trek was rewarded by the presence of two rocks, conveniently eroded by time and tide into the crude suggestion of a bench and table. They stationed themselves there and listened silently for several minutes to the crashing of the high tide against the outcrop, swirling its cooling briny foam around their grateful feet, encroaching further into their sphere, surging into their weary spirits. They leaned back on extended arms, soaking in the liberating sensations of this liminal world, a place between land and sea, not belonging entirely to either, yet holding the beautiful promise of both.

When they'd drunk their fill of the ocean, Shelton unzipped the cooler bag and began to work on opening the petite mollusks, expertly prizing-open the narrow end with a sharp jab and quick twist of his pen knife, then swiftly gliding the blade around the black-rimmed crescent of their chalky-white shells, he deftly severed the abductor muscle liberating the soft grey delicacy, awash in its briny liqueur, then slurped it into his upturned mouth.

"Mmm…a taste of the sea!"

After taking a few shots of the oysters and sea, Lidia offered to open the sparkling wine, twisting, then pulling-up the pressurized cork with confidence. Shelton set out two plastic goblets for her to fill and handed an opened oyster to Lidia.

"Well, Miss Mew, the crystal may not be up to our usual standard, but there's nothing finer, than supping off Neptune's china…down the hatch."

They slurped their tasty treasure appreciatively, then turned their attention to the bubbly.

After a thoughtful pause, Lidia asked, "Why are these oysters so small Shelton, barely more than three inches long, are they immature?"

"No, that's the breed, Beausoleil, from the Miramichi Bay in New Brunswick. Because of the way they're raised, they form nearly perfect, uniform shells, just right for a cocktail size. Their taste is subtle, slightly briny, with a hint of baked bread, don't you find?"

"Yes, they pair very well with the champagne," Lidia observed, ready to consume her third oyster.

"Yep, lovely name, 'beautiful sun', with a nice deep cup for slurping too. Did you know that male oysters acquire a tiny parasite which eventually castrates them, so they stop putting energy into reproduction and focus instead on growing nice and plump?" asked Shelton.

"How ironic! What an unsexy life for a renowned aphrodisiac," Lidia exclaimed.

"Yes, too bad for them, but so good for us," Shelton concluded as he pitched the empty shells into the sea. Then turning to offer his companion another, he was suddenly confronted by two warm lips on his own, intent on a deep and passionate kiss, Lidia put a hand on his collar, drawing him in towards her.

Dumb-founded, Shelton tightened his lips and gently withdrew from Lidia's impulsive embrace, then single-mindedly returned to opening more oysters.

"Oh, I'm so sorry, Shelton. I just got carried away!"

He kept his eyes down and silently focused on

the task at hand, not knowing what he should say.

Lidia peered at him closely, "My god, Shelton, you're actually blushing. Is it because I'm married?"

"Partly and partly because, well…I'm gay!" he declared, turning to see Lidia's reaction.

"Gay? Are you *sure*?" she said incredulously.

"As sure as I can be. I thought you knew. I just assumed everyone in our office does."

"No, I just thought you were one of those, you know, metrosexuals," she said with a slight wince.

"No, I am a homosexual. Okay, so I don't march in the Gay Pride Parade, have nipple piercings or wear a rainbow flag tie, but really Lidia, have you ever known me to be linked romantically with a woman?"

"I, I just thought you were a very private person…oh Christ! I feel like such an idiot. Are you sure *everyone* else knows?"

"Pretty sure, you want me to take a survey when we return?" Then leaning back, he suddenly broke into a fit of laughter.

"Oh, Miss Mew, and you seem *so* sophisticated! I think you are an endearing little naïf." Shelton observed his companion's growing embarrassment and laughed all the louder and harder, bringing tears to his eyes.

Lidia, unable any longer to stand Shelton's mirth

at her expense, leapt-up and stomped angrily away towards the car. When Shelton finally composed himself, he quickly packed-up and followed Lidia, who was sitting half out of the car, trying furiously to brush-off the stubborn sand clinging to the bottoms of her feet. After removing a few cloths for himself, Shelton tossed her a small box of wet wipes from the glove compartment, for which she grudgingly grunted a thanks.

Except for the quiet background music of the George Michael c.d., they drove most of the way to their motel in silence. Finally, it was left to Shelton to warm the cool atmosphere hanging between them.

"You know, Miss Mew, if I were ever to get 'a leg over' with a lady, that lady would be you," he offered with a grin.

"Yeah, well…whatever." she responded peevishly, her arms folded across her chest, eyes focused resolutely forward.

"Oh, c'mon now, don't be like that. Is there anything that's bugging you on the home front? Nick being negligent in the care of his dearly beloved?"

"Absolutely not! We are a *very* devoted couple. Now who's being naïf, Shelton? Making a big issue of a little impetuous peck inspired by too much champagne."

"Exactly, it's the Neptune effect; oysters, the sea

and too much bubbly, easy to get carried away. So... all better now?" Shelton said, flashing his charming smile, hoping for a quick conciliation, as they had the evening and most of tomorrow to get through before catching their late flight home.

But he hadn't accurately gauged his companion's anger and embarrassment, the depth of which surprised Lidia herself. She acquiesced to accompany him to the dinner club, gave her meager meal of a tossed salad and lobster roll a perfunctory taste, then, feigning fatigue, beat an early, hasty retreat to the motel.

EARLY THE NEXT morning, over a take-out coffee and bagel at a nearby Tim Horton's, Lidia announced that she had changed her flight for an earlier one, as she wanted to get back to attend to some family matters, reasoning that all that was left in the itinerary for Halifax that day was lunch at an historic brew pub and a wine tasting at Bishop's cellar, commitments Shelton could easily handle solo.

Shelton decided to feign nonchalance at being abandoned when what he really felt was a growing annoyance at Lidia's petulance. Nevertheless, he deposited her at the Lord Nelson Hotel in Halifax in time for her to catch the shuttle to the airport, it being better, he reasoned, to leave her to her own devices than to have the enjoyment of his afternoon encumbered by her surly presence.

Lidia made it in good time to check-in for her 11:30 a.m. flight, which was mercifully a mere two hours in the air, getting her back on home soil by 12:30 p.m. Eastern Time, gaining an hour travelling back from the Atlantic time zone. She couldn't wait to peel-off her travelling clothes, have a relaxing whirlpool bath, put on some Bach, order her favorite Thai food, and tuck into the New York Times, awaiting Nick's return.

But it was more than her travelling clothes she had a burning desire to shed; as Lidia sat in the half-empty departure lounge scrolling through her emails, she felt a growing sense of remorse and anxiety creep over her. She wished the entire weekend could be wiped away. *Oh shit!* Lidia thought, *what have I done?*

Shelton and she were confederates, yet it seemed their connection wasn't as close as she supposed, and she wasn't as astute as she thought. *I don't think I know anything anymore,* she lamented. The weekend had been quite a revelation for them both. *Just please god, don't let him say anything to anyone at the office;*

*no, he had more class than to do that...*she hoped.

Nevertheless, Lidia worried that her tipsy lunge at Shelton meant her marriage was in trouble. She loved Nick, she was sure of that, it was just that over the years, their union lost the romance and passion she needed. Then looking up from her phone, she caught the silhouette of a young, expecting couple; the girl's eyes closed, head on her lover's shoulder. His free hand gently, protectively, resting on her heavy belly.

A memory emerged in Lidia's mind; she, full and ripe again, lying naked, Nick spooning against her, his hands reveling in the hard roundness of her belly, luxuriating in the warmth of her full, milky breasts; nudging his desire against her, urging himself within her and not a word between them, only sighs and moans; hot breath on the nape of her neck, adoring kisses on her shoulder; passion flowing between and through them, like manna...from heaven.

An intrusive, urgent voice rasped over the intercom, "Passengers on flight 221 to Toronto, proceed to boarding at gate four."

The image quickly faded, Lidia sighed and rose slowly, making her way to join the herd.

FLY ME TO THE MOON

WHILE LIDIA SAT in the back of the cab speeding down the Don Valley Parkway towards the emotional refuge of her matrimonial home, in her well-appointed kitchen a highly amplified Frank Sinatra crooned the suave refrain *'Fly me to the moon and let me play among the stars.'* Aldo, dressed in his new paisley, silk dressing gown, belted-out in his rich baritone, "Let me know what life is like on Jupiter and Mars," as he artfully arranged some olives, a few cold cuts and slices of cheese for the snack he prepared, to share with the owner of the lovely soprano voice and fulsome figure pouring their wine.

Then as if on cue, the two turned and crooned together, *"In other words, darling kiss me!"* and they did, to the surprise and horror of Lidia who stood undetected in the kitchen doorway.

"What the hell is going-on here and who *are* you?... You bimbo!" Lidia's furious indignation spat out of her mouth like a piece of rancid fish, "Uh, and is that *my* dressing gown you have on? Oh, I don't believe this!"

The startled pair tried to regain their composure, Aldo's buxom blonde companion cowered behind him, grasping his upper arm as if in fear of a charging bull. Aldo's mouth hung open and his face was flushed, when suddenly his own sense of self-righteous indignation rose to match that of his furious daughter's.

"How dare you call my friend a bimbo, you just watch your mouth Lidia, she's a lady… your cleaning lady to be exact. I guess, 'Ms. High and Mighty', you don't recognize your hired help unless they're on their hands and knees!" he challenged, thrusting out his chest.

"VOULA? You mean you're having sex with *my* cleaning lady, dad – how dare you!" Lidia yelled pointing an accusatory finger at her father.

At this, Aldo advanced a few steps towards his daughter, his companion taking the opportunity to hide on the other side of the kitchen island, well out of the firing line, while Aldo launched into an indignant harangue.

"Waddya mean, 'how dare you?' Dare to what? Be a natural human being, with natural needs and desires, to be a man? You think, you're the only one who needs passion? Think you and your generation created sex, do you? Well, I'll tell you something, missy, I created you. Yes, me!" he emphatically jabbed a stubby finger into his chest, "I AM A CREATOR!"

Shouting on, he raised his arms above his head, his robe pulled wide open, accidentally exposing a

Viagra-induced erection. His stunned and speechless daughter flew up the stairs, shrieking, as if pursued by Lucifer and all his hellish minions.

IT WAS A little past midnight when Nick mounted the unlit steps to his darkened porch and fumbled with the key in the lock, finally it turned, and the door opened to admit him into a pitch-black hallway. Groping for the light switch he called, "Hi! Hello! Lidia? Aldo? Anybody home?"

Flipping on the switch, the sudden flood of light revealed a note tacked to the newel post written in an angry scrawl, *I'm gone with Voula and won't be back! A.C.* Nick deduced that *A.C.* was his father-in-law, but who was this 'Voula' he's staying with, and why? And where was Lidia?

Feeling puzzled and weary, he decided to pursue further investigation from the comfort of his bed, so he shouldered his travel bag and headed upstairs, where he found his fully clothed wife lying rigid on their bed, a glass and near empty wine bottle on her bedside table.

"Cara?" Nick said quietly concerned, standing over his expressionless wife, "Are you alright?"

"No," came the dull response from the prone

figure staring blankly at the ceiling. Despite lying still as death, Lidia suddenly felt the room spin, "Nick," she whispered, "is the room spinning?"

"No cara, the room isn't spinning."

"Oh…are you spinning?"

"No, I'm not, it's just your head," he reassured her.

Sitting on the edge of the bed, facing his wife, he picked-up another empty bottle from the wastebasket, and holding it up to the light advised, "I think you had better try to sit up…slowly, okay?"

"Okay, will you help me, Nick?"

"Yes cara, I'll help you."

He got hold of both her forearms, "Now, on the count of three, I'll pull you up, ready? One, two, threeee! There."

"Oh god!" Lidia put a hand to her mouth, made an urgent heaving sound, Nick sprang quickly out of the way, as his wife, bent over, ran to their bathroom and in one violent retch, emptied the contents of her stomach into the toilet bowl.

After tidying-up both his bathroom and his wife, tucking her into bed with a Gravol, a cup of weak tea and dry toast, he donned his pajamas and decided to put himself, and the whole bewildering incident to bed, to be dealt with in the morning, when he might get a more coherent response from his wife. And so,

Nick put out the light, grateful to be left in the dark, at least for a few restful hours.

THE NEXT MORNING over more weak tea, a poached egg and toast, a still shaky Lidia related her shocking discovery to a bemused Nick.

"My father thinks he's god almighty," Lidia began.

"Well, he's always been a little full of himself, if you don't mind my saying so," Nick commiserated.

"No, I don't mind, in fact he thinks he's 'The Creator'!" Lidia screeched in exasperation, then reached for more Tylenol, as her head began to throb.

"The Creator? What do you mean? Just please, tell me plainly, what happened between you and Aldo yesterday."

"Okay!" and with that Lidia launched into a graphic and somewhat exaggerated account of the already astounding event.

"So, you got a gander at the family jewels, which I concede is pretty traumatic *and* discover he's having it off with 'Voulez-Vou-lah' eh!" he intoned provocatively, leaning back grinning, pleased as much with his father-in-law's amorous exploits as he was with his own clever wordplay.

"Oh great, so he's a big hero in your books now, all lads together, nudge-nudge, wink-wink. I wish I'd never told you now, you don't understand the gravity of this situation, Nick!" Lidia shouted sternly, immediately regretting the effort as she winced in pain.

"Grave situation, what grave situation?" Nick mocked as he poured himself another coffee. "The man has a girlfriend, so what? Are you gonna read him the house rules? Ground him for having an illicit sleep-over? Or perhaps we should find out if they're having 'safe sex', we wouldn't want a shotgun wedding now, would we?"

COFFEE, CRULLERS AND CONCILIATION

Despite Nick's apparent nonchalance over Aldo's relationship, Lidia set him the quest of retrieving her prodigal father, persuading him to return to the bosom of the family, where his wary daughter thought she could keep an eagle eye on his comings and goings. Nick knew from experience that resistance was futile and so had no option but to comply with his distraught wife's request, he being propelled by a subtle reservation of his own about the whole affair.

A stubborn two weeks later, Aldo agreed to meet his daughter's emissary at the Coffee Time Donuts near Voula's apartment. When Nick arrived, he saw with relief that Aldo was alone and already installed at a corner table, nursing a hot coffee, beside it an untouched cinnamon cruller perched on a pristine paper napkin. Nick waved hello and waited at the counter to get his order of hot chocolate and maple glazed donut, a forbidden sugary treat.

"Well, long time no see. How've you been, Aldo?"

"Oh, can't complain, and you?" he said casually, taking a bite of his cruller.

"Me? I'm good, but your daughter's pretty upset."

"Lidia? What's she got to be upset about, now that I'm out from under her roof, my life's my own." He leaned back in his chair and shrugged.

"Well, that's actually the crux of the problem, Lidia misses you, we both do, Jesse too. We want you back under our family's roof, where you belong. It's your home too, Aldo."

Nick leaned on his forearms, searching Aldo's eyes for a sign of conciliation. Aldo looked down at his hands, "My home too? Sometimes it just doesn't feel like it, with 'Miss High and Mighty' laying down the law to me. I'm an adult, her father, where's the respect?"

"You're right, sometimes she comes down too hard, but it's only because she worries about you. And what happened two weeks ago, that was a mistake; I know you thought you had your privacy and that there'd be no harm done. I'm sure you're both a little embarrassed about it, I know Lidia is. You shocked her and she over-reacted, but you can see it from her side, can't you? After all, she had no idea you even had a lady friend."

"Alright, if I'm to come back, some things'll have to change," Aldo said warily.

"Of course, I'm sure we can come to an agreement that will give both parties their privacy," Nick assured in his most amicable tone.

"Okay, sounds good to me. Listen though, we can usually go to Voula's, it was just that her place was being painted and since you were away, well…"

"The mice can play? I understand," Nick said with a chuckle.

"So, when can I tell Lidia her 'prodigal father' will return?"

"Today suits me, I have my bag packed, we can pick it up right now."

"What's the rush? Things not going smoothly between you two?"

"No, we're fine, it's just that I like my independence and she cooks too much cabbage. It stinks-up the apartment and gives me gas, and the three cats, I can stand for a bit, but I don't believe in keeping pets that do their business in the house. Give me a dog any day; at least they don't shit where they sleep, so to speak."

As Nick drove his father-in-law home, he couldn't resist prying a little into the mysterious charms of 'Voulez-Vou-lah', as he came to think of her.

"So, Aldo, tell me about Voula. Since she started cleaning for us two months ago, I haven't had an opportunity to exchange more than a fleeting greeting."

"Voula? Well, there's not too much to tell. She's originally from Ukraine, fifty-two, divorced with a married son and granddaughter in Michigan. She's been in Canada for thirty years. Originally, she was working in geriatric care, but after a few years, she decided to get out of it, too depressing and she didn't like the bureaucracy, so she became an entrepreneur.

"You know she has twelve other cleaners working for her, all immigrants. She trains them, and ensures workmen's compensation, decent wages, hours and working conditions. She does small commercial as well as domestic premises.

"She's a smart gal, a real go-getter, with an interesting side-line as well." Aldo said, pleased with his image of Voula's talents and the interest they raised in his son-in-law.

"A sideline, eh? What sideline is that, Aldo?" Nick, ever more curious now, took the bait.

"She's an on-line astrologer and psychic, does tarot readings too. Has her own channel on You Tube, AstroVoula, sixty-thousand subscribers," he said proudly.

"Really? Are you into that hocus-pocus?"

"Nah, it's just an amusement for me, but don't tell Voula that, she's really sincere about the influence the cosmos has on our lives. Her web page has a birth chart calculator. You just enter time, date, place and year of birth, then you get all your major planetary influences," Aldo said, his hands shaping an imaginary celestial sphere.

"All of them? I thought everyone had only one astrological sign." The esoteric in Nick was now roused.

"No, that's just from newspaper hacks, real astrologers look at your sun, ascendant and moon signs to get the full picture. Take Lidia for example, she's a classic sun in Virgo, anxious, detail oriented, critical, controlling, with a Libra ascendant, seeking balance and harmony in the home, and beauty in her surroundings as well as her person. Then her emotional aspect, a moon in Cancer, definitely a rule-the-roost home-body."

"How do you know all this?" Nick asked intrigued.

"Easy, I had Voula do her chart!" Aldo laughed.

"I still don't understand why you're interested in her astrology channel, Aldo."

"Oh, that's because she also gives your weekly lucky lotto numbers."

"Any good?" asked Nick.

"Actually, not bad. So far her picks do forty-five percent better than my random selections do."

"Really, well who would've thought?" Nick shook his head in surprise.

After Nick helped Aldo settle-in back home, he set about making lunch for them both when Lidia called, "Well, is he back?" she asked impatiently.

"Yes, thank-me very much," admonished Nick.

"Sorry, thanks Nick. Hey, did you get a chance to speak to her?"

"You mean Voula? No, Aldo was alone at the coffee shop and I waited in the car while he fetched his things."

"You know Nick, I have half a mind to fire that

hussy," Lidia declared.

"Just leave well enough alone, will you. After all, the house is clean, right? She does her job, doesn't she?" reasoned Nick.

"Oh yes she does, and more. She does way too much more!" Lidia shot back.

"I know. But I bet she and Aldo have a lot of fun together polishing our kitchen floor," Nick laughed.

"Oh, thanks a lot for that visual," Lidia groaned.

"No problem." With that he rung-off, a little pleased with the slight consternation he had caused his still-indignant wife.

THE LIVIN' IS EASY

LIFE IN THE Ponti household progressed smoothly over what was left of the summer. Jesse and Josh were now a couple, a development which Lidia and Nick witnessed with some relief, taking it as a sign that their daughter had finally put the 'Ainsworth incident' behind her and was reconciled with Athina.

They watched their headstrong, serious daughter evolve into a more light-hearted young woman as she spent time with the affable Josh, who despite being six years Jesse's senior, seemed boyish and fun.

They spent an energetic week camping, hiking, and kayaking in Algonquin Park, activities which the reluctant 'courier-de-bois', Jesse, was learning to enjoy, as she could now appreciate The Group of Seven's landscapes with a fresh eye.

Up to now, her closest encounter with the great outdoors was during adolescence, when she and Athina spent a few weeks each summer at a posh Art camp by a pastoral lake in upper New York State. Algonquin Park was a far more rugged experience entailing challenging encounters with foraging black bears, wading moose, marauding raccoons, Josh's beef jerky chili, the stench of greasy mosquito repellant, peeing in the bushes and sleeping in a musty tent. Yet despite these travails, the pair felt a growing romantic attachment as they conquered the Canadian Shield together.

After summer school was over, Lidia and Nick took themselves off to Quebec for two weeks, first exploring the bucolic scenery, artistic and gastronomic delights of the Charlevoix area on the St. Lawrence River's beautiful North Shore, then a second sojourn at a friend's cottage outside of Baie-Saint-Paul, where they swam and sailed, a relaxing time they both enjoyed immensely.

Voula and Aldo enjoyed having the house to themselves and even decided to take a five-day trip to Atlantic City where they watched a boxing match, saw an amusingly hokey magic show, ate copiously from the groaning buffet tables at their hotel and almost broke even at the slots and blackjack tables.

After that, they had what Aldo felt was a welcome break from each other as Voula went to visit her son and granddaughter. Although Aldo was happy with the sex and companionship his relationship with Voula provided, he was used to being solitary and to live in his own way, according to his own whims.

Chapter Four

AUTUMN

THE HOLY GRAIL OF FUDGE

WHENEVER NICK FOUND himself in a funk, he turned to the consolation of his favorite confectioner's dark chocolate walnut fudge, its divinely creamy texture, the contrast of slightly bitter chocolate spiked with sweet crunchy shards, veritable little jewels of amber walnut brittle made his heart sing and all the world seem a much better place. It relaxed him no end, and today he was determined to crack the recipe that he so coveted but was hitherto denied.

On this cool, golden September morning he tied-on his freshly laundered, white apron, arranged a mise-en-place of his best copper pans, spoons, spatulas, candy thermometer, scales, and precious ingredients. The battery was charged in the tiny tape recorder Nick used to record lectures and compose his thoughts, this time to record the notes of his culinary experiment. He was resolute that today he would capture the holy grail of that illusive, perfect fudge recipe or expire in a diabetic coma trying.

The swoosh of dry ingredients being shoveled out on the scales; the rhythmic chopping of the chocolate; the gurgle of cold cream streaming into the measuring cup; the sugar bubbling into a pool of molten amber; the focused attention of Nick's five senses on the actions and reactions he set into motion; the concentration each step required quieted the worried voice in his mind.

Lidia had just bid him adieu, to attend mass at Frank's church, then lunch with him at the rectory to discuss a project he had in mind for them, the invitation being fortuitous, as she knew better than to hover over her husband when he was like this, anxious over the prostate exam he faced on Tuesday.

Lidia advised Aldo and Jesse to similarly make themselves scarce, giving Nick some space in which to work-off his apprehension with solitary immersion in his favorite past time.

By eleven-thirty, Nick's first test batch had set, it wasn't bad, pretty good in fact, if you didn't know to what the chef compared it; but it was slightly gritty, some of the sugar having crystalized, the texture a little stodgy and the taste a tad too bitter. He reckoned he could palm it off on the grad student T.A.s, if their predilection for hideously over-spiced, greasy chicken wings, pizza loaded with rubbery cheese and mystery meat donairs were an accurate barometer of their gustatory discernment, then they would love it, nevertheless, he decided to attribute its creation to his wife, if anybody asked.

Two hours and two test batches later, Nick sat by a crackling fire, ensconced in his favorite wing chair, feet-up on the foot stool, two squares of perfect dark chocolate walnut fudge and a small glass of tawny port at his elbow. From the stereo, the divine Miss Ella cooed to him over her little lost basket. Life was good he decided, licking his fingers with smug satisfaction. He had cracked it! The comfort of the world's best fudge was his to summon from his fingertips, what bliss.

Lidia entered through the back door, and surveyed the stacks of gooey pans, soiled implements, encrusted cook top, mucky backsplash and sticky countertop despoiling their usually orderly kitchen. On the table there were three different colored plates of chocolate walnut fudge, each displayed artfully in a pyramid, the only semblance of order to be found at what looked like a violent culinary crime scene. She picked-up a piece of fudge and followed the music to her living room where she found her husband, relaxed and seemingly happy.

"Had a good day then?" she asked.

"Excellent, and you?"

"Very good, the sermon was inspired, Frank was in fine form. It was nice to have the opportunity of a long chat with him. Did you know he was writing a cookbook, *Of Hearth and Vine*?"

"Yes, he mentioned it; sounds an interesting project."

"I thought so. He's immersed in researching how religious practices and values influence food culture, taking as elemental examples bread from the hearth and wine and beer from the vine; you know hops and grapes. Anyway, they're all fermented products, historically and chemically related. The best bit is he asked me to do the food styling and photography for it! I accepted of course, so long since I've been able to flex my artist's muscle."

Then taking a bite of fudge Lidia exclaimed, "Mm... oh Nick, this is wickedly delicious!"

"You think so? From which plate did you get it?"

"From the blue plate, why?"

"Oh, that's the first batch is all. Anyway, I'm glad you like it," then underneath his breath, "seeing as you made it."

"What?" Lidia asked.

"Oh nothing, let's eat out tonight," Nick suggested.

Then considering the chaotic state of their kitchen, Lidia affirmed, "Oh yes, let's."

A FORTNIGHT LATER, Nick and Lidia sat side by side, anxious and attentive in Doctor Armstrong's consulting room.

"Nick, how have you been since your exam? Any change in your urinary functioning, any further mishaps, still waking-up a few times each night to urinate?"

Nick nodded his head and felt a déjà-vu of shame when as a seven-year-old bed-wetter he was posed the same questions, "Yes, but not every night, I've been doing the exercises you recommended and that seems to help…and no, no mishaps."

"Any pain when urinating, or blood in your urine?"

"No, no, never," Nick responded, shaking his head.

"Good, and erectile function? How is that doing?" the doctor looked from husband to wife.

Lidia answered, "Actually we haven't been active lately."

"Oh, and why is that Lidia?"

Shit, she thought, *I should've kept my trap shut and let Nick deal with this one.*

"Well, we've both just been tired I guess, and

more than a little apprehensive about Nick's test results. Did you find anything of concern doctor?" Lidia asked, impatient to steer the exchange away from their sex life and towards the issue of Nick's test results.

He picked-up on his cue, "Nick, your p.s.a. which is prostate specific antigen, is slightly elevated, but that isn't conclusive of anything. I'd like you to have a few more blood tests over four weeks to establish your baseline.

"The digital exam revealed a rather enlarged prostate, enlargement isn't unusual in a man of your age, Nick. But I'd like to have a urologist examine you. His office will call you when they have an appointment scheduled."

Nick and Lidia nodded in comprehension.

Walking hand-in-hand, they made their way to the parking lot.

"Well, that's okay then. Isn't it, cara?" smiling, Nick squeezed his silent, worried wife's hand.

"Is it? We didn't exactly tell the doctor the whole truth, now did we?"

"Oh, c'mon, I'm fine. Why do you always have to look for the black cloud in the silver lining eh?"

"Don't do that, this is serious, Nick!" she pulled her hand from his and shoved it in her pocket, "I don't like that Dr. Armstrong just dismissed your p.s.a. results like that…I've been doing some reading and actually anything above zero is cause for concern."

Nick stopped dead in his tracks, turned on his wife and shouted, "For chrissakes! I'm fine! Why must you go on and on? There's nothing wrong with me. So why don't you" …he glowered menacingly, … "Just shut-up about it!"

They both stood still, frozen, as Nick stared defiantly down at his admonished wife; resigned, hurt, turning her back on his anger, Lidia made for their car. They took their seats beside each other, the only sound, the click of seat belts, their tacit ritual, securing them against unforeseen disaster.

POPPYCOCK

For years, Thanksgiving was a feast the Ponti family and friends usually celebrated in town, rotating to whoever was willing and able to accommodate their extended family feast. But now the children had grown, giving thanks for their own youthful pleasures elsewhere, apart from their parents, and within their own extended urban families.

Now the long-time friends were free to relax and celebrate the feast in a laid-back way, this year, at Paul and Becky's cottage in Muskoka, just outside of Huntsville. The ancient, rustic retreat, originally a sports-mans' camp, had been in Paul's family for three generations and now devolved to Paul, the last of his great-grandfather's male progeny, the last male of the Deauville clan, who with three daughters had little hope of passing-on that pioneer, northern Ontario Francophone name, unless in a hyphenated form.

When Becky suggested they sell the camp, as when on the rare occasion they had time to go up, the girls usually wanted to stay in the city, Paul refused. He loved the place, it was the locus of so much that was happiness in his distant, carefree childhood, a wondrous heritage he made sure his little girls experienced in every season.

So, no matter where they later chose to live in this sophisticated glass and concrete world, he was determined that the sweet sap of Canadian maple; the elegance of silver birch; the morning quaver of lonesome loons; the beaver huts flooding the marsh in spring; the sting of mosquitoes in summer, snowshoeing on the lake, lit by the eerily brilliant Wolf Moon; all this would be etched deep in their psyches. Inexorably calling them, whenever they needed to be, right back here in their spiritual home.

THIS YEAR, PAUL, a skilled bowman, had bought his tags for the season's deer-hunt, invited Javi and Nick to join him. Frank's parish duties amongst the shut-ins, kept him in town. Although Javi and Nick could not legally join the hunt with Paul, they were happy to accompany him, Nick never having been on a hunt was eager for the experience, and Javi who had hunted moose in Newfoundland, but never used a bow, was interested in observing its technique.

Early dawn saw the men up, finishing a hearty breakfast of fried bread, sausage, eggs, and strong camp coffee. Eventually, Becky and Lidia straggled-out to the kitchen in sweatpants, hockey socks and thick, Cowichan sweaters, warmed themselves by the old iron stove and prepare decent brew from the Bodum. Then, they saw their men off as they climbed into their wellies and camouflage gear.

Lidia and Becky stood on the steps of the screened porch, waved, shouted encouragement and cheeky queries re: their husbands' life insurance, then returned to the warmth and comfort of their respective bedrooms, hugging mugs of soothing java and a clutch of glossy magazines.

After a cozy lie-in and a light breakfast, Lidia

took a walk, gathering the last of the Michaelmas daisies, devil's paint brush, wild rose hips, mountain ash, wild apples and assorted fall foliage to adorn their Thanksgiving table.

Becky stood at the kitchen sink, peeling the last of the root vegetables she would blanch, then scatter around the roasting turkey. Lidia put the finishing touches to the table arrangements, pleased with what her artistry created, grouping the floral material with the additions of small colorful gourds, crab apples, pinecones, and Virginia creeper along the length of the harvest table in three old transfer-ware vegetable dishes, their crazed glazes darkened by generations of use.

The effect was rustic and homey and went well with the triad of bees-wax candles firmly anchored in the middle of each arrangement. The well-worn, buff cotton table linens, edges embroidered with faded images of resplendent ruffled turkeys and horns of plenty, completed the vintage vignette.

The two long-time friends were a study in complementary contrasts. Lidia was sophisticated, self-possessed, a little vain, and not too much of a feminist to exercise her feminine wiles in getting her way. She was outspoken and quick-witted.

While Becky had a quiet confidence and reticent demeanor, often mistaken for shyness, Astro Voula would pronounce her the quintessential Scorpio of whom the saying 'still waters run deep' was aptly applied. She moved quickly and spoke slowly, in a low husky voice, her mouth in repose often settled-into a subtle smile, as if she were listening to the whisper of some secret inward genie.

Becky was the eldest of seven siblings, from the tiny settlement of Ilfracombe, just outside of Ravenscliffe, in Muskoka. She and Paul met when she was working summers as a maid at The Bigwin Inn; Paul was there for five weeks laying new floors. They were instantly smitten with each other and responded enthusiastically to their mutual, physical attraction with the result that they were married that fall, Becky being only seventeen and two months pregnant. She went on to have two more children, twins, making it three in all, by the time she was twenty-two. Over twenty-three years of marriage she helped her husband build their lucrative flooring business, learning the trade inside-out, laying floors with him in the early days when they were short-handed. She organized their domestic affairs efficiently, without fuss or drama and kept her three daughters in line with a quiet, firm discipline.

But however much Becky seemed emotionally 'together', so 'in control', Lidia's instinct still made her suspect that there was something deeply troubling her friend and in Lidia's own, deceptively innocent way, she was determined to find out what it was.

When all the preparations were done for the evening's celebration, Becky and Lidia retreated to the comfort of the wrap-around screened porch. The interior was flooded with warm, late-afternoon sun, it's chipped and peeling window sashes framing an idyllic view of flaming fall colors and sparkling water.

Becky stretched-out on a thick, faded floral print cushion slumped over the wobbly frame of a green wicker divan; Lidia curled-up in the matching chair and ottoman, a bottle of Veuve Clicquot, two flutes and a tin of Poppycock caramel corn on the floor within easy reach between them.

As Lidia thumbed through a stack of *Cottage Life* back issues, searching for inspiration for features, Becky topped-up their glasses.

Then, before popping a cluster of caramel corn in her mouth, she inquired, "So, how's the new job going? Being editor must be interesting, calling the shots, creating your vision for each season."

"Huh, more work, but not much more pay," chortled Lidia.

"Yeah, but at least it's work you love, and it is a promotion, more clout, more prestige, no?"

"Sure, I love the work, but it's not like you, running your own business, being your own boss, creating something that's uniquely yours and Paul's. That's gratifying."

"It used to be, but everything becomes just a job after a decade or two. Except for Paul, it's still his pride and passion."

Suddenly aware that this was the little fissure in Becky's smooth façade that she was looking for, Lidia put down her magazine, sat a little upright and before raising her glass to her mouth, turned to Becky. "What do you mean, *except* for Paul? Weren't you always passionate about it too, I mean all the sacrifices you've made, the hard work, surely you love the business?"

"No, I never loved the business, Lidia, I loved Paul… I was never passionate about it, I *was* passionate about Paul." Becky let out a little hollow laugh and casually tossed more caramel corn into her mouth.

Lidia was stunned at this assertion.

"What do you mean *was*? Are you saying you don't love Paul anymore?"

"Oh, I guess I love him, I'm just not 'in love' with him, if you know what I mean, haven't been for years." Becky took a deep gulp of Champagne and watched, slightly amused, as Lidia let the information sink-in.

"Does he know? Oh my god, are you leaving him?"

"Yes, and yes. Paul's a nice man, a good father, but he's not right for me anymore. Look, I was a horny seventeen-year-old hick, flattered by his attention and wildly attracted to his dark good looks. He cut such a cool romantic figure for a kid like me, remember he fronted a band, had a sexy voice?"

"Oh yeah," recalled Lidia, "when he sang, 'Stand by Me', every girl in the audience curled her toes!"

"Well, my toes haven't curled for years," Becky said, ruefully.

"Oh, c'mon Becky, every marriage has its dry spells, every flame, its flicker," challenged Lidia. Then a glint of insight flicked across Lidia's eyes. "Ah-hah! You're having an affair, aren't you?" Lidia leaned across to her friend conspiratorially. "Spill, lady!"

Becky laughed "Oh Lidia, it's not what you think…yes, I've had an on-again, off-again fling with someone I've known for ages. He's fun, interesting, and sexy. And if anything, having him in my life helped keep me in my marriage for longer than I wanted. He was an ill-considered diversion, is all."

"You've known him for years? Who is he?" Lidia asked warily.

"Javi."

"Javi!... Javi?... you mean OUR JAVI? *Are you nuts?*"

The words were barely out of Lidia's mouth, when she leaned over too far, missing the arm support for her elbow, and landed with a thud on the wooden floor....

"Ouch!... shit, that hurt!" Lidia shouted rolling on her side, then sitting upright, she cradled her tender, bruised elbow.

Becky, laughing, stood up and extended a long slender arm, helping her injured friend to her feet.

"Are you okay, Lidia? Oh god, you should've seen the look on your face!" Becky deposited Lidia back into the armchair, then went to fetch a cold compress.

"Oooh, it's too cold!" Lidia protested as Becky secured the compress with a knotted towel.

"Just keep it there for a bit, then you won't swell and bruise so much."

"Are you sure it's not broken?" Lidia worried.

"Naw, if you can move it, it's not broken," assured Becky.

After regaining her composure, Lidia was determined to dig deeper, "Okay. So, what's your plan then, move in with your Latin lover? What about the business? What about your girls?"

Lidia winced indignantly, through more than a little pain.

"No, you don't understand Lidia, I'm not leaving Paul for Javi. I'm leaving him, well, I guess for myself."

"Oh, right, to 'find yourself', how very sixties of you!" Lidia said, smirking.

"Okay, that's enough… do you want to talk properly, or just go directly into 'the shame and blame game' because you disapprove?" Becky said leveling her most no-nonsense gaze directly at Lidia.

Chastened, Lidia calmed down a little and decided to listen to her friend, who obviously needed to get this off her chest and if she couldn't give her approval, then perhaps she could at least offer understanding, after all life wasn't black and white, no matter how easy that would make it.

"Sorry Becky, go on. I really do care, you know," Lidia reached for her friend's arm.

"I know, that's why I want to talk to you. Honestly, I wish I could stay in the marriage and not disrupt my family's life, I really, really do. But I can't ignore the fact that more and more I've grown not to like myself very much."

"Why? You're a great mom, caring friend, capable businesswoman," Lidia asserted, hoping that this might just be a mid-life self-esteem issue.

"Why? Because I'm a phony, a fraud, not only to Paul, every time I pretend to be interested in what he thinks and feels, or to enjoy sex with him, but also to myself, every day, when I pretend that I care about what I'm doing and that preserving my material comforts and polishing that thin veneer of a 'happy family' is worth sacrificing self-fulfillment for.

"All those things, a beautiful home, prosperity, they're just a palliative to ease the pain of what's going-on inside me. I've realized that everything I truly need now is within and not outside me, I just have to recover that treasure."

Lidia stared intently at her friend.

"Well, it seems you've done a lot of thinking about your feelings, but what about the more mundane considerations? Aren't you worried about the girls, the business, your income? How do you propose to support yourself?" Lidia frowned.

"Kate's almost finished her degree and wants to go on to grad school, there's more than enough money for that, and the twins, they're not academically inclined, and want to join their dad in the business, something Paul is delighted with and quite frankly, I'm relieved by. I guess for selfish reasons.

"You see, Paul is a relationship kind of guy, not at all a lone wolf, he thrives when surrounded by people who share his passion and want to learn. He's a natural team-builder and teacher, with far more patience than I. We're blessed that Monique and

Danielle, from adolescence, liked to help-out in the business, in whatever small way.

"Monique is really interested in marketing and Danielle is great in customer service, they're willing to take courses specific to improving the business, but they're not abstract thinkers; like their dad, they're all about application," Becky observed, smiling.

"Okay, but what will you live on, or for that matter do?"

"I have retirement savings, own half that business and half our home too, you know. But I wouldn't ask Paul for a buy-out right away, we'll have to work something out for the time being. I plan to rent something cheap and cheerful in a convenient location, then start work on getting my travel agents' license."

"You're thinking of opening a travel agency?"

"No, not right away at least. Sally Curzon and I have been talking about going into partnership."

"Oh, Sal Curzon, the gal who started the cycling art history tours of Europe in the eighties. I hear she's expanded into other niche markets, quite an innovative businesswoman."

"Yes, she is. I've interested her in developing vacation experiences for the professional, single woman or retired female solo travelers. We'll offer select, sophisticated cultural activities, interesting ecological excursions and appropriately challenging sports, in safe, upscale venues where they're treated with respect and not bothered by unwanted attention, condescended to or addressed as 'dear'."

"That's a very marketable concept, one whose time is certainly overdue," Lidia acknowledged.

"It is. You know I got the inspiration at your New Year's brunch while chatting to Anne who travels a lot, is single and still gets the 'Oh my, all by yourself, dear?' from waiters when dining alone, no matter how much she can plunk down for a meal. The number of single women with healthy, disposable incomes is growing. The marketplace had better sit-up and take notice, as these female consumers are discerning and have economic clout, something the banking, real estate and car industries are only starting to realize," Becky said, proud of her insights.

"But that still leaves the question of your relationship to Javi, to say nothing of his with Paul," observed Lidia.

"Well, as for Javi and I… I cut that off last year, even though he did want to go public with it and have me move in with him. You know, he's not nearly as self-possessed and cynical as he pretends, deep down, he's quite vulnerable and more than a little needy."

"Huh, I'd never have guessed. How'd he take it?"

"I'm not sure really, he seemed fine, but like most men, he's good at hiding his feelings. The sticky part is, do I tell Paul? On the one hand, I don't want him to think Javi is the cause of our split, yet I want for once, everything to be above board, no more living a lie." Becky shook her head resolutely.

"Tough call kid, but I think that'd kill Paul. He's always been a little jealous of Javi's class and sophistication. Just think of the hurt he'd feel knowing you were unfaithful; he idealizes you, you know," Lidia said softly, looking away.

"Well, it's time that he grew-up and came down to earth. Anyway Lidia, I've suspected for a while, that when he does contracts out of town, he isn't laying more than floors himself! In any case, until things are finalized, please keep this to yourself, not a word to anyone. When Paul decides to tell his friends, is his call. Agreed?"

"Agreed," Lidia sighed and gave her friend a sympathetic hug. Just then, their attention was diverted toward the gravel road, and the sound of Paul's SUV, pulling an ATV trailer, rounding the corner into the drive.

CURRY AND COVER BLOWN

ALTHOUGH JESSE OPTED to stay in town with Josh for the Thanksgiving weekend, she saw little of him until Sunday, as he claimed to be buried in research for an end of term engineering project, then at the last minute on Saturday night, he was called-in for a shift at the corner shop where he worked part-time. But now at last, they had some time together, to watch the *Bourne Identity* for the umpteenth time.

They never failed to laugh hysterically every time Matt Damon was called-upon to say the French name, Marie (*Mah-rreee*), which he consistently mispronounced as 'Murray'. This became a little inside joke, the kind that young, newly allied couples have before petty grievances elbow the romance out of their memories and time transforms delightful ritual into dull habit. And neither of them wearied of the thrilling car chase through the streets, back alleys, and steps of Paris, inspiring them to plan a summer tour of the continent in a rented mini-Cooper.

While Jesse paused the movie, just before the car chase, Josh phoned in their take-out order of butter chicken for him, shrimp Vindaloo for her, with side orders of steamed rice, masoor dal, vegetable pakoras, naan, and raita. As Josh concluded the order, Jesse returned to the living-room, cum-bedroom of Josh's compact bachelor apartment with a tray bearing a bowl of Bombay mix and two glasses of Strong Bow lager.

Before Josh could press the button on play, a loud, insistent rap echoed from the front door. Jumping-up in surprise, Josh peered with one eye out of the peephole to see his father's belligerent expression looming menacingly close to the aperture, his mother standing just behind him, apprehensively clutching her over-sized purse, the parallax optics making them seem two terrifying 'fun-house mirror' specters intent on invading the peace and sanctity of his cozy hidey-hole.

Aww!…Hi! Mom?…Dad? Josh opened the door admitting his parents, sounding as confused over their identity as he was about their presence in his home. His father, followed by his mother, pushed past him without returning any greeting, then stood planted resolutely in the middle of the floor, grimly surveying their surroundings, taking-in the untidy scene.

Rumpled duvet and pillows were piled high in one corner, the hiking boots, skates, cross-country skis and poles leaning against another, the computer station and a large LED screen mounted on the wall opposite the sofa bed. Their eyes finally rested on the startled, silent figure of a pretty, young woman about to put a hand-full of Bombay mix into her gaping mouth.

"Well, Joshua, where's your manners boy, introduce us to your young friend," commanded the short swarthy intruder, staring fiercely at his host.

"Oh, sure! Um…mom, dad, I'd like you to meet my girlfriend, um…um…." Terrified, Josh suddenly tongue-tied, wrung his hands and looked for the name he needed somewhere on the ceiling, a nervous tick he acquired when as an adolescent stutterer he was called-upon to address the class.

Jesse stood, wiped her greasy hand hastily on her jeans, and extended an open palm, "Hello, I'm very pleased to meet you Mr. and Mrs. Patel, I'm Jesse Ponti."

"Please dear, call us Miriam and Sudhi…lovely to meet you too!" Miriam said brightly, shaking the girl's hand and giving her husband a slight nod, indicating he should match her warm greeting, a cue he ignored, preferring to keep a silent face 'like thunder'.

"Please, sit down," Jesse indicated the couch and moved toward Josh who finally recovered his speech.

"Yes please, do sit…um, can I get you something mom, a cup of tea?"

"That would be lovely, dear."

Jesse, two steps behind Josh, whispered, "What's going-on? I thought your folks were in Montreal, and why do you look so guilty? What've you done?"

"I can't explain now, I have to go back in there, *please* come with me."

"Oh no way, your dad is steaming. I'm going for a walk while you straighten this out." With that she grabbed her jacket and beat a hasty retreat down the hall, Josh calling after her,

"Oh, please Jess… let me make this up…I'll call you!" he implored, as she disappeared into the elevator.

"Joshy, never mind the tea dear, daddy and I need to talk to you. Please join us."

Josh sat in the computer chair opposite his parents. "So, how did you find me?" he said quietly to the folded hands in his lap.

"Is that all you have to say? What is the matter with you boy? Hiding from your parents like this…huh, well it's no wonder you want to hide, considering all the lying and thieving you've been doing!" Sudhi Patel shot the accusation out furiously at his frightened son.

"Now Sudhi, that's a little harsh, look you're frightening the boy."

"Boy? Boy? Miriam, he's a man for God's sake, or he should be. Stop babying him, woman! Now explain, boy or I'll…I'll…"

"You'll what, dad?" Josh challenged calmly, meeting his father's gaze.

"I'll lay charges against you for fraud, that's what!" he shouted, jumping-up to shake a finger in his son's face.

"Now, Sudhi, that's quite enough. Sit down and compose yourself," Miriam said, sternly.

"There will be no nonsense about pressing charges against our own son and I will thank you to remember, Dr. Patel, that I contribute equally to his education."

Straightening her jacket and her posture, Miriam Rosen addressed her son.

"Now Joshy, you will tell us why, when we attend a medical conference at the university and decide to stay-on through the long weekend to surprise our son, we find that *we are surprised* when none of the professors in Engineering have seen you for over a year, and that your cousin, with whom you claimed to be sharing a room in residence, tells us to ask at 'The Dep' for your whereabouts.

"They in turn direct us to your address here. So, it seems we should've named you Waldo, as in 'Where's Waldo?' Eh? So, Joshua, what have you been doing all this time with your life *and* the money we gave you for education, room and board?"

"I've invested it," he said, leaning his elbows on his knees.

"Oh god, don't tell us you've lost it in Bitcoin, you fool," said his father.

"No, no, nothing risky like that. I invested it, and the money bubbe and zayde left me, in my own business dad…in 'The Dep'…I actually bought it!" he declared smiling, sitting back, satisfied with himself.

"You bought a corner shop, with all your inheritance and tuition instead of completing your engineering degree? You think that's some kind of achievement, do you? Something to be proud of do you? Don't you realize that's what they all do, the over-qualified and desperate who come here to the 'land of opportunity' and find that every profession in which they were fully qualified back home shuts its doors to them, closing ranks to protect their own. Trust me son, no one comes to Canada with dreams of owning a depanneur… a tawdry corner shop!" shouted Sudhi.

"Well bubbe and zayde did pretty well in their dep…they were happy, mom grew-up in it. And when I was young and you were both too busy with your own careers, you were happy enough to let them raise me there too," he countered.

"I knew no good would come of leaving our only

son with your parents to babysit. Women's Lib is all very well, in its place, but none of this would've happened Miriam, if you stayed at home with your son, instead of trying to be a high-powered businesswoman!"

"Oh, shut-up Sudhi! Really dear, you can be such an idiot, do you think the money for medical school and the down-payment on our first house just fell from heaven, eh? No, it was from the little dress shop I owned and spent all hours of the day at, and the next shop and the next, until I was established, and we could live comfortably until you got your residency. So, don't throw Women's Lib up to me!"

"Oh, that is a typical exaggeration of the facts my lady, you know very well that down-payment came from my Auntie Jaswinder!"

"Hah! Really Sudhi, do you think that Jazzy's measly…"

"That's enough, you two!" shouted Josh, jumping to his feet.

"It's always about *you*, even when I really wish it *wasn't* about *me*… Oh god…what am I saying?" he flung his arms above his head in exasperation. "Look dad, I know you want the best for me, and to protect me. But, I can't conduct my life perpetuating your notion of social advancement.

"I appreciate what you do is very important dad,

but honestly, how many people in their lives will actually need a brain surgeon? Whereas everyone, every week, needs bread and milk, a trashy mag, a Kit Kat or a Kinder Surprise and most of all a connection…to greet their fellow human beings, their neighbors and sometimes on a slow Sunday, just to hang-out and shoot the breeze."

"Oh, so that's what you're running on our hard-earned money, eh? A drop-in center for neighborhood losers!" Sudhi shouted.

"Oh no, dear," rejoined Miriam. "You mustn't let the local layabouts ruin the tone, you should focus your efforts on satisfying the *paying* customers, Joshy. Didn't my parents teach you anything about retail trade?" Miriam shook her head in chagrin.

"As a matter of fact, they did mom; they taught me about being part of a community that takes care of the less fortunate, old and isolated. Bubbe always, especially in winter, kept an eye on her 'oldies', the regulars who lived alone with their cats, she had a grapevine and would call or go around herself with a little care package if no one had seen them for a while. Zayde'd sometimes pay me pocket money to deliver or shovel their steps and walks. Well, I try to do that for my people too, I put soup, sardines, bread and milk on sale nearly at cost the week before the pension cheques are out, because that's when the pensioners are running low."

"Really, *at cost*? Well, you're no Galen Weston, now are you?" scoffed his father, looking in disgust, away from his son.

"Who's 'Galen Weston', dad?"

"Never mind Joshy, daddy is just having his bitter little joke at your expense, take no notice," consoled Miriam.

"That's it, I've had enough of this silly badinage. Miriam, get your purse, we're going," Sudhi announced, standing up just as the delivery man arrived with Josh's take-out.

"Oh, who can that be knocking, Joshy?" Miriam asked.

Then without skipping a beat his father retorted, "Well, you can bet your boots it ain't opportunity." With that, his father made for the door, pushed past the delivery man, and stomped out.

Miriam lingered while Josh paid for his take-out.

"Oh dear, I hope we haven't spoiled plans with your lovely friend, Jenny."

"Jesse, mom, her name is Jesse."

"Yes, that's right, Jesse. She looks a very nice girl, Joshy. I like her."

"Thanks mom, she is, but you've only met her for a minute."

"Never mind, a mother can tell. And look, you

can make this good with daddy, just put together a business plan, show him you are a serious and responsible person. Do a flashy spreadsheet, can't you? It doesn't have to be terribly accurate; your father knows nothing about these things, just make it look good, okay? And bring home Jenny for a weekend, we'd love to get to know her better, darling," Miriam said, patting her son's cheek, smiling affectionately.

"Okay mom, thanks…love you!" he said, as he gave his mother a hug, then waved her off down the hallway. Josh shut the door and let out a sigh of relief.

"Oh… Jesse!…Oh, shit!, shit!, shit!" he cursed, searching the sofa cushions for his cell-phone. "Hi sweetie," Josh greeted her innocently, "Oh no, *please* come back…I can pick you up right now, oh *please* sugar-puff, your favorite shrimp Vindaloo is here. Okay, stay where you are, I'll be right there!"

Later that night, after Josh and Jesse had eaten their curries and were curled-up together in the sofa bed, Josh explained his duplicity to Jesse, who lay naked beside him.

"So, you see that's why I had to lie to you, just for now, until you met my folks, so you wouldn't have to lie to them for me. It was bad enough that I had to lie, but I now know that was stupid, just forestalling the inevitable."

"It was pretty brutal then?" Jesse looked up at Josh, concerned.

"Actually, not as bad as I imagined it would be, after mom convinced dad that he really shouldn't try to put me in the slammer for fraud. He compared me to some geezer named, Galen Weston, whoever he was, probably some 'King of the Corner Shops' back in the day."

"Whoever he was, you can bet the comparison wasn't flattering," Jesse snorted. "Anyway, your folks should be glad you've found something you love".

"Well, that's not *everything* I love."

"No? Then tell me, Joshua Patel, what else do you love?"

"Me? Well, I *looove* your tits… they're so beautiful, warm and round and firm." He ran his hands over one, gently squeezing as he neared her, "delicious little raspberry nipples."

As he licked them, she giggled happily and wriggled with delight, then pulling him closer, as she opened up to him, firmly guiding him into her she whispered, "And Mr. Patel, do you know what I love about you?"

"Oh, please tell me," he murmured.

"Everything. Absolutely everything."

Aldo and Voula made themselves scarce over the Thanksgiving weekend and the two weeks beyond, spending time together in the sumptuous abode of one of her clients, who was off to Palm Beach for a few weeks, leaving his trusted cleaning lady to house-sit, one of the few perks of her business.

The sprawling 'Prairie House-style' cedar beam, stone and plate glass home was nestled in a large, wooded lot in the tony Bridle Path area of Don Mills, the first planned Toronto suburb. It subtly integrated a variety of housing and community services with commercial and light-industry sites, while preserving a quiet sense of gracious country-living, incorporating many cul-de-sacs and public spaces such as ravines, parks, and greenbelts.

The exclusive Bridle Path enclave was originally an equestrian farm, Windfield Estates, owned by E. P. Taylor, a brewery magnate with a passion for thoroughbred horses out of whose stables emerged the legendary Northern Dancer, the greatest racehorse and sire of the twentieth century.

E.P., as his friends called him, was an early adopter of the gated community, a concept at odds with the architect of Voula's employer's home,

Arthur Erickson, a pre-eminent visionary whose planning philosophy influenced the design of the suburban community of Don Mills in the 1960's. The idea of an exclusive gated community, being antithetical to liberal Canadian social values.

Aldo, clad in a borrowed sumptuous navy-blue velour bath robe, sporting a Royal Canadian Yacht Club crest on the breast pocket, concluded a call on his cell phone and was headed towards the whirlpool when Voula emerged from the indoor lap pool. "Who was that Aldo?"

"Number-one granddaughter, wanting me to help-out with Nick's surprise fiftieth birthday bash."

They both stepped naked into the swirling vortex of the hot-tub's bubbling, turquoise mineral water, her employer being a firm believer in its salutary effects.

"A surprise party, eh? Well, that's nice, but Nick's a Scorpio with Taurus rising; they don't usually like surprises; they like to be in control and know what's happening next. Just like their ancient symbol the bull, they don't change direction easily, unnerve them though, then it's horns down and full steam ahead," Voula warned.

"It'll be fine, no worries with Nick, he likes a good party and lately with his health issues, he deserves one."

"Well, if you say so," conceded Voula, pressing her back against one of the jets, spreading her legs and arms, tilting her head back. "Oh, God that's so good. My body is getting too old for all this housework, bending, kneeling, reaching, scrubbing…they can invent all the fancy-schmantzy electronic tools they like, in the end, it's all down to 'scrub, scrub, scrub'! A woman's work is never done."

"Waddaya mean, 'woman's work'? You employ men too, don't you?" challenged Aldo.

"Yeah, but I prefer not to as they're lousy at it, difficult to train and don't stay long," Voula asserted.

"Listen lady, it's a known fact that men's work, over the centuries, has been harder; we built the pyramids, never mind Stonehenge – that was a real killer without the wheel.

"Then it's off to war, marching for miles with heavy backpacks, pulling cannon or sailing the treacherous seas, 'row, row, row' that open boat… man those Vikings were tough bastards." Aldo leaned back, satisfied with his argument.

Voula sitting-up now, crossing her muscular arms across her chest, replied, "Oh really? Just who do you think was left at home to fend-off 'those tough bastards' with a crop in the field to harvest, babies to suckle, eh? Who was protecting your hearth and home, while you were out rowing your boat all over the Atlantic, eh? We never got to see the world, like you did!" she scoffed, and looked away.

"What, do you think it was a vacation? 'Disney's Wonderful World of War' perhaps? Anyway, we went on tilling the fields when we got back home. That's *if*, we got back home!"

"Oh, shut-up," laughed Voula.

"No, you shut-up," Aldo laughed back.

"C'mere, you miserable man and give me a kiss!"

Just as he put his hands on her thighs, leaning over to fulfill her command, he muttered, "Uh-oh…"

"Oh god, Aldo, what is it?" Voula said, alarmed.

"Oh boy, I think I just weed in the whirlpool."

SAKE, SUSHI, AND SECRETS

AFTER BECKY'S STARTLING revelation and the subdued atmosphere that hung over the rest of the Thanksgiving weekend, Lidia was grateful to return to the emotionally neutral territory of work, where she busied herself training the new intern in managing *Your Best Life's* various social media accounts. But, her emotional safety-zone was soon breached by Shelton, who she discovered in the lunchroom giving a surreptitious good-bye peck on the cheek, to none other than Clive Snodden, Brunhilde's P.A., spy, and general dog's body.

This time it was Shelton who was embarrassed as his editor stood silently before him, eyes wide, with an accusatory smirk on her wondering face.

"Ah! Hail Miss Mew! Well met!" he bluffed and blustered.

"Oh really? So, you're glad to see me, are you? Any news you'd like to share… *friend*?" Shelton winced as if afflicted with a sudden pain while trying to exit gracefully, but Lidia was too fast for him, stepping back quickly, closing the lunchroom door, she leant against it, one hand securing the doorknob, "Oh no you don't, mister! You'd better start blabbing now or I'll tell everyone what your first name really is!"

Shelton stepped back, resigned, "Alright, Clive and I are seeing each other… anything else you care to know?" he said, adopting a casual attitude, inspecting his French manicure.

"You bet…how long, how much do you pillow talk and why, for God's sake, why Shelton, are you, my confidant and stalwart, sleeping with the enemy?"

"Oh, Miss Mew it's not like that! Pillow talk, really what do you take me for? Anyway, he's not at all the enemy, he's very simpatico and I will have you know, my liaison has rendered some very interesting reconnaissance."

"Oh yeah, such as?" Lidia challenged.

"I'm not at liberty to divulge that now...all in good time, my pretty," Shelton teased, in an effort to relax the mood.

"Well, it had better be good! But really Shelton, what can you possibly see in that guy, he's so...so...Uriah Heep!"

"I deeply resent your comparison; he is nothing like Dickens' odious creation. In fact, he is warm, funny, a gourmet cook, and has the most adorable, chubby, furry little..."

"*ACH, NO!*" Lidia covered her ears, "Too much information, for god's sake!"

Shelton pulled her hands down, held them fast against her sides then mouthed uncomfortably close to her face, "*shihtzu*"

"Oh?" Lidia said, uncertainly.

"It's a dog, stupid!"

"Ah," responded Lidia, with relief.

Shelton quickly seized the opportunity to pull the door open and bolt from the room.

TOO ANTSY TO stay behind her desk at the office and

apply herself to more mundane tasks, Lidia called her good friend Siobhan Moran, their food columnist on a hiatus at home, testing recipes for the second edition of her darkly humorous cookbook, *Killer Cook*.

As luck would have it, Siobhan was available today, as her work was being interrupted anyway by the antics of her seven-year-old twins, Dylan, and Dara on a school break for teachers' P.D. day.

A good laugh and gossip with Siobhan was just what she needed right now to ease the tension, so she left instructions with her intern to advise all who asked for her that she was away from the office doing research. Then off she went to visit her friend, stopping along the way to pick-up a couple of Bento boxes for their lunch.

Siobhan and Declan Moran had the prescience to leave Southern Ireland before the 'Celtic Tiger' lost all its teeth, choosing the soil of the politically and financially stable Dominion of Canada in which to plant the seeds of their family's future. Declan was a real estate broker with Sotheby's; Siobhan, a cookery writer, blogger, and broadcaster; professions which travelled well.

Once they were established in the vibrant city of Toronto, Canada's multi-cultural center, they started their family, beginning and ending with their precocious identical twin boys, Dara and Dylan, a delightful duo, but a challenging handful for all but the saintliest parents.

AS LIDIA WAS putting-out the plates, chopsticks, napkins and ponzu sauce, her host warmed the sake in the microwave, then turned toward the island counter, only to be startled by a strange and sudden apparition.

"AAAH! Dear God in heaven! What is *that*?" Siobhan shrieked, confronted with a huge bobbing yellow grapefruit on a meat fork, sporting her mother-in-law's hair-switch tied-on with a silk scarf, beneath it, a terrifying smear of crimson lipstick surrounded a gash, set with ferocious dentures.

"It's Granny Grapefruit, mom!" shouted two very excited voices from beneath the other side of the counter.

"Granny who?" Siobhan said, a hand fluttering on her chest. "Look, I won't have you two abusing the food in this house!"

Oblivious to their mother's distress, the twins turned to each other, "Let's go scare granny with it! Yeah!" They raced out of the room, a blur of long blond curls and flashing sneakers.

Their mother shouted after them, "Do you have *any i*dea of the cost of that fruit? And that had better not be my Chanel lipstick and new Gucci scarf – you little devils!"

Then turning to Lidia who was weak with laughter, Siobhan said, "God, how they love to torment her. Ah well, it gives the dog a break.

"You know the poor thing's got nerves so bad he has O.C.D., shredding all the bath towels, then hording the evidence in his basket, poor love. He's been for behavioral therapy, you know. A waste of time really, when Paxil's so much cheaper, and works just as well. Anyway, we only got him for Declan."

"Aah," said Lidia, "Such a sweet man, loves dogs, does he?"

"Not especially, just needs an excuse to go out for a smoke, so when he 'walks the dog', he's really just goin' out for a puff. He's not allowed in the house, you see."

"The dog?"

"No, Declan, you ninny. The dog doesn't smoke," Siobhan answered, as she raised her tiny cup of warm sake. "Slainte!" they chimed together, the Gaelic salute to good health.

As she deftly picked-up a California roll, Lidia asked, "I don't know how you handle the demands of a three-week visit from your mother-in-law, the twins, the dog, the house, Declan's crazy schedule, while revising a cookbook."

"It's not too bad really, I have a few strategies in place which give me and Declan some peace. On weekend mornings I let the twins choose a few individual boxes of those sugary breakfast cereals, you know the ones that are full of empty calories and give fat kids diabetes? Well, they get a tray with their cereals and a little shot of Bailey's for their gran and watch her early 'Corrie street' boxset in black and white with her, they love it, don't understand half of it though 'cause of the Manc accent…they think it's like Dickens," she giggled, swishing a piece of tuna in the ponzu sauce. "Then Declan and I get to have that thing married couples need once a week."

"You mean sex?" responded Lidia.

"Oh god, no! A lie-in."

They both laughed and tipped their sake glasses.

"So, granny Moran drinks Bailey's, in the morning?" Lidia said raising her eyebrows.

"Well to be fair, she probably doesn't know it's the morning, she's a bit *confused*, see. Which leads me to my second strategy. By about Wednesday and it's all been too much, at six p.m. Declan sends the kids to their room with pizza and some Disney dvd's, then I go around and close all the drapes, turn off the lights and tell her it's *very late* and time to go to bed…and off she goes."

"You don't really make her go to bed at six, do you?" asked Lidia.

"No, I'm not that mean, I wait until six-thirty."

They both laughed loudly, Lidia nearly choking on a mouthful of barbequed eel, "God, Siobhan, you are wicked."

"Yes, I know," she acknowledged, smiling.

Then suddenly pensive, Lidia asked, "But why do we do it?"

"Sleep?" responded Siobhan.

"No, I mean the whole thing…marriage, family, tying-up our young adult lives, when we should be 'footloose and fancy free' instead of working every hour of the day and into the weekends.

"Scrimping and saving so we can up-size out of our crummy little apartments and into our heavily-mortgaged homes. Then finally arrive at the point when we own the damn things, only to find that it's all too much, so set about down-sizing in anticipation of our old-age and the final down-size, into our six-by-six graves. The last piece of over-priced real estate we'll own," intoned Lidia glumly.

"Or urns…they can be quite decorative actually," mused Siobhan, resting her chin on her hand. "But I do know what you're saying; 'specially having kids, I mean what're they actually for? They're pointless really. Once you get them off your tits and out of nappies, it's about eight years on an emotional roller-coaster.

"One minute at the height of euphoria over the purchase of a couple of seedy goldfish, then despair, after creating a goldfish 'toilet-water-park', discovering that to flush them down into the bowl-slide is deadly," recollected Siobhan. "Then there's adolescence," she continued. "All hormones, spotty pustules, stinky feet and wankin'-off… which only means more bloody laundry," Siobhan complained, as the lone female amongst five brothers.

"Yeah, followed by the fresh hell of the teenage years," rejoined Lidia, pouring them another glass of sake. "God, what a stupid idea that was. Ha! Must've been invented by a man." She laughed. Then continuing her theme, "Teeny-hood, one seven-year long sulk, punctuated by petulant fits of pique and self-righteous indignation over their parents' unworthiness to share the planet with them. Followed by their twenties during which, when they're not smirking at us, they're begging from us," Lidia concluded, heaving a sigh of chagrin.

"Thank god for work then?" Siobhan said.

"Oh, yeah…Oh! That reminds me," Lidia said, brightening considerably, "our cathartic moan nearly made me forget the other tasty thing I brought besides sushi – fresh gossip!"

Getting-up to warm more sake in the microwave, Siobhan said over her shoulder, "Do tell sister, I'm all ears."

"Well…," Lidia waited until her friend was sitting across from her, pouring more sake, "Guess who Shelton Avery is dating? Give-up?" she asked dying to break the news. "Only Clive Snodden!" Lidia exclaimed, anticipating Siobhan's reaction.

"Get out! Snotty Snodden? You must be joking…please tell me you're joking! What does our dishy Shelton see in… *Cliiive*?" Siobhan exaggerated his name in disgust.

"Well, apparently he's got an adorable shihtzu, which I think is the chief attraction."

"A shihtzu, eh? Can't stand them meself, I like a dog that looks like one, you know, with a long, cold wet snout, to goose all your female friends with." They both laughed at the familiar experience.

BEER AND SYMPATHY

PAUL WAVED-OFF THE waiter's offer of a drink order, preferring to wait for Nick, who was late. It had been a while since Nick and he had a chance to have a relaxing lunch at their favorite bakery-bistro, ComPanis. A neighborhood institution, with an ochre stucco facade sporting a green and white striped awning, its wheat sheaf logo carved into a large wooden baker's peel, hung horizontally above the battered oak door.

Inside, the decor evoked an Italian country bakery, more stucco on the interior walls, vintage pendant lighting hung from an unpainted, pressed-tin ceiling; well-worn terra-cotta tiles lined the floors. The tables were various shades of marble with belle-époque wrought-iron pedestals.

A vintage, carved wood and brass rail bar ran a third of the length of the long, narrow space, its ornately framed mirror having lost some of its silvering.

Rustic wicker bakers' baskets lined the walls, overflowing with the day's crusty, flour-dusted loaves. At the back, there was an open-kitchen of brick wood-fired ovens where aproned pizzaioli worked their Vulcanic alchemy.

It must be at least three months since we got together here. Thanksgiving sure didn't give us much chance for a tête-à-tête. What a weekend, no luck bagging a deer, just missing a damn beautiful six-point buck. Then dinner table atmosphere as fun as an old aunt's funeral. God! I shouldn't have downed so much brandy afterwards, he reflected with a heavy sigh, as if still feeling the hang-over. *Well, I'm glad Nick texted, it'll be good to talk.*

Just then, his friend boomed from behind him, "Hey, Paul! How's it going?"

"Comme ci, comme ça." Paul made a hand gesture indicating equanimity. "And you, Monsieur Ponti, or should I say, 'the late' Monsieur Ponti?"

Nick pulled-up a chair opposite his friend, "Sorry Paul, held-up at the nursery, you know how it is, noses to wipe, butts to kick. A minder's job is endless," chuckled Nick.

"Well, better you than me. I have enough of a time with the Hecates."

"Oh now, you have great girls, hard workers, no grief and they adore you."

"Yeah, I know, we're both blessed… in our kids at least," said Paul, ruefully.

"Oh, things somewhat short of heaven on the matrimonial front, Paul?" Nick asked concerned, leaning heavily on his forearms, eager for his friend's response.

"That's an understatement… huh, you do know about Becky and me splitting-up?" Paul said, raising his eyebrows in surprise.

"Splitting-up? You and Becky? God, I'm sorry, I

had no idea! Why am I always the last person to know these things? I feel so stupid."

"Hey buddy, don't feel bad, forget it. I just thought that might be the reason for the lunch invitation, you know, for beer and sympathy?" Paul said, giving his embarrassed friend a reassuring pat on the shoulder.

"Sure Paul, if that's what you need, that's what you'll get. Waiter," Nick raised his voice and gestured for service. "A Stella do you Paul?" Paul nodded. "Two Stella's then, and lunch menus please."

As Paul recounted the domestic drama he was currently facing, Becky resolute to move out of the matrimonial home next month and his suspicions around her motivation, Nick struggled to give his friend his full attention, but found it wandering instead to the imminent health issue occupying his mind.

"She says she's not seeing anyone, but I don't believe her. My gut tells me otherwise, I just wish I knew who the bastard was. I'm not saying I'm a saint, I've strayed a little, but only lately and more for comfort I guess, and ego, than the actual sex, even though that was an attraction, seeing as Becky doesn't care for my attentions anymore.

"But I'd never leave her for anyone else-I still

love her as much as I ever did. And I want to keep my family together, those are the values I was brought-up with and I stick by them," asserted Paul as he cut into the thick crust of his pizza.

"That's a tough one, Paul. I don't know what to tell you, Becky says she's leaving because she's unhappy with her life, but there's no third party, eh? Well, I guess you have to accept her word and her wishes.

"Leave the lines of communication open. Leave her to spread her wings, if that's what she really needs, she'll thank-you for it, may even come back to you in time. In fact, I think there's a better chance of it if you loosen the ties, not try to tighten them," counseled Nick, taking a deep swallow of cold beer.

"Okay, maybe you're right. I'll go along with it, just to keep peace, for the girls' sake. But I still think there's more to it than a mid-life crisis," Paul hailed the waiter and ordered more beer for them both.

"Hey, speaking of mid-life crises Nero, I seem to recall you'll be celebrating a milestone birthday next month, fiftieth, isn't it?"

Nick rolled his eyes, "Oh, please don't remind me, or anyone else for that matter. And I'm definitely not celebrating the fact," Nick said as he drained the last of his beer and plunked the glass down with conviction.

"Oh c'mon! You've got to have a party, 'push the boat out'. Javi, Frank and I'll do the catering; that is if I can get a hold of Javi, the illusive prick – he owes me money, I suspect that's why he's gone to ground. Silly man, it's not like I don't know where he lives." Paul smirked.

"Maybe he's out of town. Look, anyway I don't want a party; I mean it, not even a cupcake with a candle. I put Lidia on notice not to plan *any* surprises. I just can't face it," Nick scowled, leaning back, folding his arms across his chest.

"Whoa, that's a little harsh – what's the matter?"

Nick thought for a long moment before deciding to speak, "I don't feel like celebrating for two reasons Paul, first because I have to have a biopsy on my prostate in three weeks and it's weighing on my mind, a bit," Nick blurted-out his news to his astonished friend.

"Wow, that's … terrible…I don't mean terrible in that it will turn-out terrible, I mean terrible that you have to go through it, but you'll pass with flying colors. You're a healthy guy!"

Nick just looked down and shrugged.

"What's Lidia say? You know women, always on the internet researching, or watching The Doctors, most of 'em talk like they've earned a medical degree. I'm sure she's got this in perspective, no worries,"

Paul assured, trying to inject some optimism into the atmosphere.

"Lidia doesn't know," Nick said quietly.

"What!" Paul raised, slightly, out of his chair, at the declaration. "Are you crazy? Why won't you tell your own wife? That's something that should be shared between you. She has a right to know!"

"I know, that's why it's weighing on me," Nick acknowledged, looking-up, feeling guilty. "I never keep secrets from her, but this is different. If I tell her, I know she'll only go on about it, like you say, researching on the internet, badgering the doctor, meaning well, but giving me no peace. Don't want the drama.

"And every time I look into her eyes, all I'll see is worry, the worst outcome looming there, and I'll get mad, then she'll be hurt and go quiet. I've already yelled at her once over it; I just lost it. I'm very ashamed of that," he confessed, feeling a little better having expressed his misgivings to his friend.

"I think you have to do what's best for you right now. After all, this is about you, but maybe this isn't the best way of dealing with it, honesty being the best policy?"

"Perhaps, I'll think about it. I'd like to find a way around Lidia discovering my 'sin of omission', I can't imagine what would happen if she did."

"Oh boy, then you'll *really* have some drama!" Paul's eyes widened, as he shook his head at the thought. "So, what's the second reason, Nick?"

"The second reason is, I hate having to 'celebrate' my birthday, because every year, I hoped my mom would come up from Rochester to celebrate with me. And every year, she sent me an expensive present with a cheesy excuse, I just stopped wanting to hope, and got over it." Nick hailed the waiter, ordering another round.

"Yeah, your aunt Sonia's idea of a fun birthday party was one greasy hotdog, one slice of cake each with one scoop of ice cream, a lame game of Snakes and Ladders, then out you go! Frank's were pretty low-key too."

"Except for that time his mom took us all to Pizza Hut, then paid for our passes to the all-night horror flicks at the Willowdale Odeon," recalled Nick.

"Oh yes, I remember. D'ya think maybe she had a hot date that night and wanted us out of the way?" asked Paul.

"If so, it was a hot date with a Bingo card," Nick laughed. "Yours were pretty wild though, your mom just stocked the rec room bar with all kinds of pop, bowls of snack food, stacks of games and we could play the stereo loud. Her two rules before closing the door, 'no necking, no fighting'."

"Yeah, my mom was cool. Remember Uncle Raymond used to get pissed, burn the burgers, then sneak us some beer through the basement window?"

"Oh yes, two reasons your birthday parties were popular was the beer, then getting to play 'spin the bottle' with your older sister Lucille, she was really cute. In fact, all four of your sisters were cute, and sweet," Nick grinned at the memory.

"Sweet? Hell-cats more like," Paul said, laughing.

"Oh c'mon, like you weren't mama's favorite. But Javi's parties were the best, Imelda really knew how to throw a bash. His confirmation party was legend. Remember? It was a pool party with a D.J., and what a spread."

"That was a great asado, barbequed suckling pig, potatoes and peppers roasted in the dripping. Mm, I can taste it now, first time I had suckling pig, and the last time I had it so good," Paul licked his lips at the memory.

"I agree. Before she died, I begged her for the recipe, but she wouldn't budge. I guess she wanted to be remembered especially for it," Nick said, his eyes a little misty.

"Yep, I guess we all want to be remembered, for one special thing at least," agreed Paul.

MANY HAPPY RETURNS

IT WAS ELEVEN o'clock on a Sunday morning in mid-November when Lidia, Javi, Aldo, Jesse and Josh were deep in collusion, notepads, checklists, and hi-liters at the ready, planning for Nick's fiftieth surprise birthday party.

Lidia sat at the head of the kitchen table, large-square calendar in front of her. "Okay, so Javi, you and Aldo will get all the fish on Saturday?"

"That's right" Javi said, "then we'll get the dressed salmon and ceviche done at my place, we'll also pick-up all the breads, I have lots of baskets for the tables."

"Good," said Lidia, "It's always better to have a few different food stations spread-out around the room, so people don't converge in one spot, forming a line to get fed. This way they'll mix and mingle, without the annoying wait. Oh, and make sure the service gives us four large *round* tables and please don't place them against the wall, I want the guests to be able to walk around them."

"Right. And the linens, plates, glasses, and cutlery are being provided by the service," Javi confirmed.

"And Paul will definitely pick-up the meat orders? Salume, souvlaki, bresaola?" asked Lidia.

"Check!" Javi said. "And he's making-up the various condiments, salsa verde etc. and Kate is taking care of all the crudo with herb oil and balsamic dips. Paul will bring it over early to my place and arrange it on the platters."

"Great, thanks Javi. And the drinks?"

"All in hand, Lidia." He leaned back, crossed his arms and grinned.

"Wonderful!" Then Lidia turned to Jesse and Josh, asking, "How's the plan for entertainment going?"

"Really well Lidia, I'm borrowing my friend's DJ gear and he's told me where I can source some old twelve-inch vinyl from the seventies club scene, so we'll have some retro scores for the slideshow, then a good dance mix to keep things lively. Oh, and I even got a mirror ball and some strobes."

"Fantastic! This is going to be so much fun. Oh, and Jess please don't forget the glow sticks," Lidia grinned, so excited at the thought of a festive, sparkling party.

"Okay, so mom, I've got the wait staff and bartenders lined-up from school. Don't forget, they'll expect cash plus gratuity at the end of the evening, okay?" reminded Jesse.

"Right, I'll make sure to go to the ATM," confirmed Lidia. "Dad, how are you and Jesse doing with the slideshow?"

"Tomorrow we'll start sorting through the boxes of photos and memorabilia you gave me, if there's someone I can't identify, I'll ask. Then we can put a timeline together, hopefully an entertaining one," added Aldo.

"Okay, but I may not know everyone either, and I can't ask Nick, so maybe cousin Dom might help if we're really stuck. You know, Nick's never even opened any of those boxes his mom left for him, he just shoved them into the cupboard below the stairs and forgot them, I guess." Lidia shrugged.

"I'm actually looking forward to going through them, mom. I'm curious. I've never even seen a picture of nonna and nonno Ponti."

"I know Jess, but please be careful in choosing the photos, keep those from his early childhood to a minimum, and focus on pictures from school days, with friends, the choir, the hockey team, then young adulthood, his first wheels etc. I think deep down, he's still sensitive about his mom and dad," Lidia warned, then checking her list. "And last, but not least, I've got the bakery delivering the cupcakes and the florist the arrangements, masses of a variety of sunflowers, Nick loves them, they're his favorite flower, they'll arrive at your place Javi, around one o'clock Saturday afternoon."

"Well, it's a good thing my loft isn't fully furnished yet, or they'd be no room for all this stuff, never mind the guests," Javi laughed.

Lidia snapped the cap shut on her highlighter, feeling pleased and confident in her plans, "Well, thanks everybody for pulling together like this, Nick needs a good party. This'll make-up for his fortieth.

"Remember? We had the restaurant booked, everyone was there, and just before the food came, Nick was rushed to the hospital with an attack of appendicitis. Unlike that fiasco, this birthday party's gonna' be one to remember."

A JESUITICAL SOLUTION

THE BISHOPRIC OF St. Edward the Confessor, in which Father Frank Kelley had ministry, was situated on a busy suburban thoroughfare. Nonetheless, it retained the aura of a neo-gothic country church. Set well back from the street, it had an ivy-covered façade of dressed fieldstone, framed by stands of English oak and red Japanese maple; it's wide, graduated flagstone steps slowed the pace of advancing worshippers, preparing them for contemplation and prayer.

The opening of the heavy, iron-hinged, Gothic doors signaled passage from the frenetic hurly-burly of Yonge Street, into the cool shadows of sacred worship's realm. In the interior, the sentinel marble font offered anointment; the Doric columned aisles beckoned, after humble genuflection, progress to the altar precinct where jeweled light from the stained-glass windows bathed communicants in an ethereal glow.

But on this Friday afternoon, the church was empty. Father Frank looked down, hailed, and waived at his waiting friend from the organ loft, where on the keyboard of the silenced pipe organ, he had just finished some fingering exercises for a particularly challenging Healey Willan piece.

Nick stood below, searching the transept for a sign of the priest, looked-up and waved back, gesturing whether he should come up to Father Frank, or whether the priest would descend the spiral stairs to meet him.

Frank descended, greeted his friend warmly, and suggested they proceed to the rectory, where he had a pan of cinnamon buns rising, an offering for that evening's meeting of catechism teachers.

"Well, this is cozy, Frank," Nick said, surveying

the improvements in the large eat-in kitchen.

"Yes, it turned-out very well, I think. Thanks to IKEA, some scavenging Paul helped me to, along with his carpenter's wizardry; it was rather gratifying, I learned a lot from him. 'measure twice, cut once', being the principal lesson."

Frank smiled at the memory, as he lifted the linen from the large pan of puffy buns and set the dial to preheat the oven. He then asked his guest if he'd like a warming snifter of brandy, the late afternoon being a cold, drizzling one.

"Sure, that'd be great. What do you have?" Nick asked, draping his coat around the shoulders of a well-worn Windsor chair, pulling it up to the rustic refectory table the priest had made from vintage, wide-plank flooring.

"Vecchia Romagna, I confess preferring it to the French brandies, which I find have too much forward alcohol, whereas the Italian brandy has a rounder, richer, mellower flavor with a sweet hint of late-harvest grapes lingering on the autumn vines," he espoused, pouring them each generous measures.

"It appears someone's been in to the 'purple prose', writing a food and drink book perhaps?" Nick teased.

"Guilty as charged, I know I get carried away. Cheers."

The men raised their glasses to each other's health then took a deep draft of the warm amber liquor.

"Oh, that's just what the doctor ordered." Nick sipped appreciatively.

"Good, now speaking of doctors, I hear you've a worrying little procedure to face in the near future," Frank said, judging it best, knowing his friend's typical reticence, to lead directly to the heart of the matter.

"Christ, can't anyone keep a secret anymore? I'm guessing it was Paul who blabbed."

"Ah well, yes and no. He didn't mean to, it just came up in conversation, you know as it does, when discussing a friend's milestone birthday and his utter reluctance to celebrate it.

"Paul just succumbed to my superior powers of interrogation. And, as far as keeping secrets goes, you'd have done well during the Spanish Inquisition yourself, but maybe not so well if Lidia, the gal you pledged to love, honor, and cherish, gets a whiff of your perfidy."

"Tell me about it! That's why I need your sage advice. Look, on the one hand I really want to unburden myself to her, but on the other, I know she'll fret, and nag me to drink wheat grass and soy milk 'smoothies', eat quinoa 'risotto', edamame humus, gluten-free pasta and pro-biotic yogurt, ad nauseum.

"I hate that muck, and whoever heard of using anything but good old creamy arborio, carnaroli or vialone nano for risotto. God, the clue's in the name: RISOtto-it means rice!"

"Course it does, any fool knows that," agreed Frank calmly, letting his friend rant to blow-off steam. "Okay, so new-age foodie stuff aside, your dilemma consists of this: you want to do the right thing and tell Lidia about the biopsy. On the other hand, you know that this will cause her fear and worry, which she will project on to you, lowering your confidence whilst raising your ire, ultimately causing a marital rift, at a time when cohesion is most what's needed for you both. Right?"

"In a nutshell, yes," said Nick, impatiently tapping the table, anticipating a solution to his dilemma.

"But really Nick, how do you feel about it? Aren't you worried at all, I mean we all hope for the best, but prepare for the worst, mentally and emotionally, at least?"

"Feel? I feel fine. I'm tired of people stereotyping every human challenge, you must say this, feel that and act this way, otherwise, the p.c. behavior police will feel uncomfortable, or even self-righteously angry. Screw them! I don't want to celebrate my age, wear a ribbon, or run a marathon, and I refuse to mythologize disease."

"Maybe people do that, so they don't make a faux-pas? Just follow the guide, tow the party-line. Those expectations are what helps society be civil," Frank reasoned, feeling that his friend protested a little too much.

"Look, there's no more reason for me to think, at this point, that I have cancer, any more than a woman does when she goes for a mammogram. Does she think, Oh god! They're looking to see if I'm sick. Or does she say to herself, 'I'm doing this to make sure I'm alright'? The choice is hers, like it is mine. I know attitude doesn't affect outcome, but I also know it determines how well we deal with that outcome, for ourselves and our loved ones."

"Okay, so no clouds on your horizon?"

"Not a one that I can see. I'm 'Mr. Blue Sky'."

"And Lidia?"

"Stormy weather, I'm afraid."

"Well then, the solution is simple. Tell her."

Nick made to open his mouth in protest.

"*But*, not until five days before the date," advised Frank.

"What? Why?" Nick was non-plussed.

"Because, then she won't have much time to

source any edamame or wheat grass, never mind learn how to work the blender, thus minimizing the worrying /nagging quotient. Okay, so she may huff and puff when you first tell her, but be the brave little soldier, women love that.

"Be upfront; tell her you were sparing her feelings. Hang your head and look contrite. It's very effective. Then you'll have turned the tables, she won't be able to vent her anger on such a courageous and pitiable figure." Frank nodded sagely.

"Uh, what if she somehow finds out earlier?" Nick knit his brow, trying to grasp the strategy.

"It can work *whenever*! Duh. Just be even more pitiable, more worried for her than you are for yourself. God, and how long have you been married?" asked Frank, slapping his forehead in disbelief.

"Oh, okay, okay, I get it…that's clever, you are good!" said Nick, wagging a finger at his savior.

"Well, it's no accident that I chose to become a Jesuit, you know. The moral reasoning that is 'Jesuitical' is as second nature to me, my friend," declared Frank with a self-satisfied grin.

"Ever think of going into politics, Frank?" ventured Nick.

"Oh constantly, but for the good of humanity, I am restrained."

They both laughed loudly at this declaration.

Then, rising to place his cinnamon buns in the oven, Frank said, "Now, drink-up, then out you go. I have buns to bake and an agenda to compose."

"That's okay; I've got to meet Lidia downtown soon. Thanks Frank, you've been a great help. I feel much better now," Nick said, as he placed his empty glass on the counter.

"Happy to be of service, just remember we all keep secrets, often for a misguided good, but a good, nonetheless. So, only those without sin may cast the first stone," Frank warned.

"Right, well I'll certainly keep that in mind," Nick assured his friend, somewhat puzzled at his admonition.

AH…SECRETS, MUSED FATHER Frank, as he leant against the back door jamb, indolently blowing smoke rings from his quotidian of a sole cigarette, *secrets-like Becky, Javi and Nick. They think I don't really have any, so I can keep theirs; just sometimes though, I really wish all my friends were atheists,* he continued in his silent contemplation, *I don't really mind about it too much, but a little passion and excitement wouldn't go amiss.*

Like the cinquecento warrior popes, talk about excitement. Those were the 'good old days', what a time to be a priest! Why can't there be a heroic, 'TV Super Priest', eh? A charismatic, handsome priest in the lead of a suspense-filled drama, 'Cross the Line', starring Father Frank Kelley, a priest who serves God and man on the front lines of Afghanistan! Dodging the Taliban's bullets, brokering peace with the local tribesmen, while fending-off the advances of doe-eyed, nubile village girls he converts to Jesus... just then the oven timer sounded, telling him his cinnamon buns were ready.

Frank stubbed-out his cigarette and as usual, missed landing it into the damp compost heap in the fallow vegetable garden, giving Mrs. McNamara, his wily housekeeper, the relish of one more cause for complaint.

THAT SAME AFTERNOON, as Lidia headed-out to meet Nick for a Friday night, early movie and dinner date, Shelton cornered her at the elevators.

"So, can I bring my plus-one or not, Lidia?" he asked sulkily.

"Oh, alright, but just please don't talk any shop. I

don't want Clive's ears burning. I need this job, I've got a kid in college remember, and an indolent and dissolute old age to finance, so behave," commanded Lidia.

"Oh, good! Well, anyway Miss Mew, he's practically family."

"What? Don't tell me you're engaged," Lidia's eyes widened.

"No, but we may move in together. And for the record, I don't believe in engagements, elopements-yes, engagements-no. They're pointless, annoying and needlessly draining of one's own, and friends' pocketbooks. Elopements, on the other hand, are stimulating, spontaneous, romantic, and equally annoying to one's friends, but ultimately cheaper for us all," asserted Shelton.

"Oh my, Shelton, I had no idea you were such a romantic, you never cease to amaze me," Lidia laughed as she pushed the elevator's down button.

"Which birthday is it anyway, his sixtieth?"

"What? No, Nick's only fifty. Why? Do you think he looks that old?" asked Lidia, suddenly worried, dismissing the open elevator.

"Oh no, take no notice of me Mew, I'm notoriously bad at judging age," Shelton lied, trying to cover his faux pas.

"Hmm, you know he hasn't been sleeping well at

all lately, up and down during the night, restless. Maybe what he needs is a nice mini break after the party. The next week maybe we could both get two days off either side of the weekend and head north to one of those lovely spa-resorts where you can get Dead Sea mud treatments, energy-boost smoothies, and a really good liver detox. I might even swing a deal, if I can cover it for the magazine," Lidia said, more to herself than to Shelton.

"Good idea. In any case, those smoothies are wonderful, Clive swears by a wheatgrass, red algae and almond milk smoothie every day. Nick should try it. But Mew, I'd stop short at a high colonic," Shelton advised.

"Well, the energy boost couldn't hurt. I can get the ingredients at the health food store in the concourse, and I think Nick has a blender stowed away somewhere," she said, impatiently pressing the button, re-summoning the elevator.

Just then, Hilda Braun, their much-feared Editor in Chief rounded the corner, halting in front of them.

"Lidia, I was looking for you, I'd like to address a few issues in the holiday edition, in say twenty minutes?" she asked, ignoring Lidia's obvious dress for departure. "Check your inbox first for my memo though, I'd like you to be prepared, I don't have much time to waste this afternoon. Unlike some, I fear."

Still holding Lidia's gaze, she observed, "Shelton, that bow-tie needs straightening." Then turning abruptly, she headed briskly towards her office.

Shelton instinctively responded to Brunhilde's command, straightening his tie, and clearing his suddenly dry throat. "Speaking of age, Miss Mew, how old do you think our Brunhilde is?"

"Oh, I don't know, judging by her laugh lines, late forties, early fifties? Anyway, I'd better call Nick, try to catch the late show instead," Lidia said, unbuttoning her coat, hurrying-off towards her desk.

"Ha! Laugh lines my eye. Nothing can be *that* funny," Shelton muttered, grimly.

EVERY PICTURE TELLS A STORY

IT WAS SATURDAY afternoon; Aldo sat at Jesse's kitchen table, surveying a spread of various old photographs, some black and white, others in color, a stack of memorabilia in a shoebox, occupied middle ground. Jesse was busy arranging more pictures, concert stubs, decals, badges, stolen restaurant menus and other souvenirs on a corkboard, composing a storyline of her father's young adult life.

"Well, that's a start; now for the mystery: Door Number One, please!" Jesse announced, as Aldo ripped the tape from the little box that Nick's mother left for him. Reaching into its depths she pulled-out a bronzed baby shoe, an old rattle with a chewed duck's head, a yellowed satin and lace christening gown. There were white and blue, candied almonds in a tulle bonbonniere, some baby photos and cards, a little clip-on red bowtie, and a 45 record of an Italian accordion band.

Then, a small white envelope, addressed to 'My dear son', the glue from its back-flap, dried-up long ago, the little glittery heart-shaped sticker curled-up, popped-off and floated to the floor. As Jesse pulled-out the folded notes within, a small black and white snapshot fell on the table, landing in front of Aldo. In it, a pretty sun-suited blonde held the hand of a stocky three-year old, the man with his arm around her shoulders was the same one Aldo had seen before: it was Tony Assunta.

"Lemme see that," Aldo immediately grabbed for the letter.

"Why? I haven't even read it yet!" Jesse held the letter to her chest.

"Because it's not addressed to you – it's addressed to Nick, so give it here!" insisted Aldo, sternly.

"Okay, okay! Geeze don't get so touchy. I just wanted to know what the mystery's all about. I am his daughter after all, and she was my nonna. They're not even *your* blood relatives, for gosh sake," Jesse made her feeble protest, but yielded to her nonno's command.

"Nevertheless, it's obviously private and maybe sensitive material, so it's best we give it directly to Nick. You'll find out everything in the end, just trust me, okay?" Aldo assured his reticent granddaughter.

"Well, if you say so, nonno. But I'm warning you, if it turns out dad is a long-lost heir to a pasta fortune, I wanna' be the first to know!" Jesse laughed.

"I promise you, kiddo." Aldo smiled, then quickly slipped the envelope containing the letter and snapshot into his shirt pocket.

AFTER DINNER, SITTING in the privacy of his bedroom, Aldo pulled the letter out from between his mattress and box spring – a precaution lest curiosity drive his intrepid granddaughter to snooping around for it. He perched his bifocals on the end of his nose, then with a quick intake of breath shook the letter open:

Dear Nero:

First, let me tell you how proud I am of you! You're a very smart boy, one who hasn't wasted his time, talent or brains on fooling around, like so many kids today. You've been a model student and an obedient nephew to your guardians, and a wonderful son, much better than I guess I deserved, never giving me a moment's worry. I used to think you were born with an old head on your shoulders! That's a compliment, I know you're much more mature and serious than me at your age. You're like Fabio I guess, just don't work yourself into an early grave like he did or let the fun in life pass you by.

I'm so sorry I wasn't around when you were little and that you never got to live with Alf and me. You must understand, I was married too young, to a good man, but one ten years older and very serious. I was only seventeen, liked to go out and dance, be with my friends, study hairdressing maybe, not settle down to housekeeping and motherhood. I foolishly thought that getting married meant I'd be looked upon as an adult, free to do as I pleased, out from under the thumb of my lov-

ing, but very strict older brother.

Instead, I ended-up under the thumb of a too serious older man. Don't get me wrong, Fabio was a good-hearted, hard-working guy who loved both you and me a great deal, but he had to have his way, run his family like he ran his business.

Which brings me to a very difficult subject, that of your real father. I don't know any better way to say it – Fabio Ponti was not your biological father, he adopted you at birth, but you are my natural son. As I said, I liked to party, go out dancing, Fabio didn't care for all that. But when his cousin came over to Canada and joined a band, Fabio let me go out with my friends to dance whenever he was playing in town, that was safe, Tony Assunta, his cousin, would keep an eye out for me.

Unfortunately, he and I had eyes for each other. I fell in love with him, and we had a brief affair, then he had to go back to Italy to take care of some family business and didn't write or return for three long years. I was heartbroken.

In the meantime, I discovered I was pregnant. I thought I would die! I was so scared of what my husband would do. But I had to tell him, when he was a teenager in Italy, he got the mumps, which left him sterile, something that hit him very hard as he always wanted children. In the end, we reconciled ourselves to eventually adopt, once his business was secure and I was twenty-one. When I told him about the pregnancy and who the father was, he was furious, didn't talk to me for weeks, so I just held my breath and kept out of his way.

Finally, he sat me down and told me what we were going to do. He would adopt you at birth, register you as his own, raise you as his own, but Assunta was never to know. If I told him he would disown us both. In those days, women and children had few rights, so I had no choice. I knew he would treat you right, you would have a good home and all the advantages Fabio could give you. I guess he felt that since his cousin had taken his wife, it was only fair he should take his child, the score would be even, and he could go on with our marriage and our lives without bearing a grudge.

No one here but me ever knew about Fabio's problem, so announcing my pregnancy was met with congratulations and nobody was the wiser. You were a beautiful little boy and Fabio adored you.

I don't know if you remember him, I hope you do, he was a good and affectionate father, it was like fatherhood had opened him up somehow, brought out the joy and little boy in him too. I was happier and felt closer to him those five years before he died, I was a better, more loving wife, I grew-up. Funny, he grew younger, and I grew older, and we finally met somewhere in the middle where happiness lived. All because of you!

But it was too short, poor Fabio. I still think back on him and feel so sad that he didn't get to see you grow-up into the fine person you are today, just like him, serious.

Still, in some part of me, I miss him, still feel the love I grew to have for him. I know I'm dying and that's hard, to watch yourself die away, get weaker, more pain, less life, but it's worse I think in some ways to go so quick, like your dad, never getting a chance to say your goodbyes. I wish you'd have come to see me more, but I guess it's hard for you too, and the palliative care ward really isn't a place for a young guy like you, so full of life.

I was hoping we could get a little closer before I died, but I can see how awkward you feel every time zia Sonia makes you come visit – I know she does, so don't deny it. I also see the anger just behind your eyes. I guess you have the right. I was selfish, I wanted to live, not be buried at twenty-three with my poor husband!

Even though Fabio left us well-provided for I wasn't allowed to live with you on my own, my brother and his wife insisted we live with them, to be safe, to avoid gossip, so they could keep an eye on me, I couldn't even get a lease or a mortgage without a male co-signer back then.

I was suffocating living with them, Sonia is so pious, you know that well, having lived with her for so long now. Every morning bright and early, out to Novena devotions, then be dragged along to say the rosary at every wake! The only social life I got was either in the church or at their club, where my brother introduced me to an endless line of old losers looking for a young 'rich widow', 'a nice obedient Italian girl'. I felt like a piece of fresh meat being dangled in front of a pack of hungry wolves.

I'm sorry, that sounds harsh, he meant

well, my brother, but that's how I felt. So, when I was allowed to visit my younger cousin, Caterina, in Rochester, I practically ran there, she was a real card, my cousin, had her own little sports car, a bright red Nash convertible.

What fun we had driving around with the top down, going to parties with her young friends, their favorite spot to meet was Alf's parents' bar, that's where I met him. He was fun, a little older and getting ready to take the place over from his mom and dad, who wanted to spend more time travelling across the country in their Winnebago.

We hit it off immediately, I was pretty good-looking in those days, he proposed, and we were married in Rochester a.s.a.p., before my brother could find out and try to stop me. It was like I was re-born, I was happy, had a life of my own to live as I saw fit.

The only regret is that I couldn't have you with me, I knew my brother and Sonia would take good care of you, I think they were relieved I left you with them, as I'm sure Sonia thought I was going to be a bad influence on you. She never approved of me.

But I missed you every day, thought of you

all the time, believe it or not, but it's true. Anyway, I'm sure you'll judge me, it's the way of youth to judge their parents, but if you can't forgive me, then at least try to understand the choices I made, and know they were made out of love for you and for life!

I've left you a good trust fund, the lawyer will explain it all to you. I want you to be secure Nero, but have some fun too, travel, buy a little sports car, drive to the coast, see how other people live, just please don't buy a motorcycle.

your loving mother,
Viviana
xxxooo

Aldo pulled the glasses from his nose, wiped the moisture from his eyes, then let out a little chuckle as he remembered seeing the picture Jesse had pinned-up earlier that day of a seventeen-year-old Nick Ponti, mutton chop sideburns, long dark hair to his shoulders, sitting proudly astride a bright red Triumph Tiger 650.

AFTER MUCH AGONIZING, wishing he hadn't even

read the letter, vacillating between ignoring, or even destroying it, weighing-up the emotional consequences it might have on his beloved son-in-law; Aldo reluctantly chose the ethical course. Like every wise gambler, he knew better than try to interrupt the course of fate, ultimately the chips must fall where they may. He decided to approach Nick the next evening, when he knew Lidia and Jesse would be out of the house, but any drama could, if need be, quietly contained.

"I'm sorry, Nick. I opened it, not out of nosiness, but because I recognized the man with your mom in the photo, in fact I know him fairly well and where he's living," Aldo handed his baffled son-in-law the little yellowed envelope bearing the letter and picture his mother left him decades ago, but which remained, until now, unread. Aldo looked down apologetically, then quietly turned and left, with a sense of foreboding.

TEARS GUSHED DOWN Nick's cheeks, blurring the upright, rounded, girlish script of a once pretty, vivacious thirty-three-year-old woman about to lose her life, reaching-out to her son, ironically, he being much older now than she, he just old enough in fact to be her father.

But who was now reduced to the stalwart youth who stubbornly refused to mourn her passing, bitterly biting back his tears as he sang her requiem and stood at her grave. Decades of denied grief overcame him; he shuddered and shook as the defenses that his obdurate anger had built crumbled, and the terrible pain and longing rushed-out.

When Lidia returned home, she found a distraught Nick, barely able to speak, still sitting in his armchair, immobile, the letter grasped in his hand, which he offered to his inquiring wife.

She sat on the footstool and read the letter, when she finished, Nick finally spoke, "Aldo gave it to me, he says he's met my father and knows where I can find him."

"Oh, Nick! What can I say? I'm so sorry," Lidia said, as she cradled her husband's head, then drew him near. Stroking the side of his face, still damp from crying, she asked, "Have you thought what you want to do?"

Nick raised his head, wiped away any lingering tears and said huskily, "No. Oh, I don't know…I just don't know!"

Then holding his anxious face in her hands, she smiled into his eyes and whispered, "That's okay. Don't worry, you can make-up your mind whenever. Take your time Nick, there's no need to rush. I'm here, whatever you decide is best. Okay?"

"Okay. Thank-you." He smiled a little back, then said, "Just please don't tell Jesse, not just yet. I need time to take this all in."

"Agreed," assured an apprehensive Lidia.

CANNOLI AND CONFRONTATION

TWO WEEKS LATER, Nick was sitting in Cheech's Buick heading for The Sisters of St. Carmel Retirement Home, a string-tied white pastry-box filled with chocolate cannoli held steadily on his lap. Nick offered to take Cheech in his car, but Cheech insisted on driving, which was probably for the best as Nick had been unable to focus properly on mundane tasks, becoming forgetful, being perpetually preoccupied with work, health issues and his late mother's revelation.

"Do you know what you're going to say?" asked Cheech, who had been filled-in about the situation by an absent Aldo.

"What? Um, no, not really. Thought about it all week…I think I'll just play it by ear."

"Good, that's probably best, Nick. Assunta isn't too well, he was in I.C.U. last week, his lungs filled-up with fluid and had to be drained again, so no drama, eh?"

"None intended, Cheech," Nick assured him.

NICK FOLLOWED CHEECH to the common room overlooking the gardens. In one corner, opposite the library area, there was a small refreshment counter, in the middle of the room, commanding center stage, a baby grand piano. Then a few club chairs, and a sofa, where two men sat expectantly.

"Hey! Guys! Come stai?" Cheech bellowed, a little too exuberantly, upon entering the room. "Stiamo bene, paesan," rasped Assunta on behalf of them both, but a quick appraisal of his general lassitude, the slightly bowed head, watery eyes, and pallid complexion bespoke quite an opposite reality.

"Bud, Cheech, I'd like you to meet Aldo's son-in-law, Nick".

Nick smiled and extended his hand to each of the two seated men, Bud rising to acknowledge Nick's greeting, Assunta, looking very frail, offered the newcomer his cold, limp hand.

"Where's Aldo?" asked Assunta.

"Oh, couldn't come today, he's helping Voula with some errands, but he thought you and Nick would like to meet and have a chat. It seems you have some 'people' in common."

The old man looked puzzled and a little wary. "People? Who's that, then?"

Cheech took this chance to exit with his friend. "C'mon Bud, there's a cribbage board that needs playing, and this time, I'm counting your cards *very carefully*."

"Okay, Cheech, you're on!"

The two friends left quickly, leaving Nick holding the box of cannoli, standing silently before the nonplussed, partially blind old man who was his biological father. Nick, guided by a sudden, compassionate impulse, sat down across from Assunta. "How about I make us coffee, we can have some cannoli and you can tell me about my father."

"UH…WHAT'S DAD DOING sitting out in the car all by himself?" Jesse queried her mom, while squinting through the peephole she cleared in the fog on the kitchen window. She wondered at the unusual spectacle of her father reclining in the driver's seat of their car, lazily blowing smoke rings from a thick Cuban cigar through his open window. Nick's eyes were closed in rapturous contemplation of Pavarotti's signature aria, *Nessun' dorma*, the tenor's soaring, imploring belcanto expanding into the warm, late autumn night air.

"Well, mom? Is he coming in for dinner or what? What's going on?" Concerned, Jesse turned to her mother who was busy dressing the salad.

"Nothing is 'going on', Jess. Your dad's just had a very trying day, one that turned-out surprisingly well, that's all."

"So, he's really happy?"

"Well, let's just say he's content," responded a smiling, relaxed Lidia.

"Okay then, I'm going out to fetch him in for dinner, then he can tell us all about it," declared Jesse, making for the back door.

"Uh, no Jess." Lidia reached for her daughter's arm. "He'll come in, in his own good time, alright? Just leave him for now. He's alright, trust me." Lidia gave her daughter a reassuring smile, then motioned for her to sit down for dinner.

THE NEXT MORNING, Nick, Jesse and Lidia were convened around the kitchen table, each fortified with a cappuccino and mini-Danish.

"So, you left this meeting with your real father, this Tony Assunta, without letting him know you are his son? But why dad, doesn't he have a right to know?" implored a perplexed Jesse, leaning over the breakfast table, searching her father's eyes for an answer.

"I know this is a lot for you to take in Jesse. It was hard for me to come to terms with. But leaping over understanding to jump straight into judgment won't help."

"Your father's right," interjected Lidia, "Jess, just let him explain it in his own way, okay?"

"Alright, I'm all ears," she said folding her arms across her chest and leaning back in her chair.

"You see Jess, in her letter my mom explains the situation she was in, caught between the proverbial rock and hard place, she had to make some very tough decisions regarding her marriage and my paternity. In the end, I think she and my dad made the only compromise they could to keep their family together and provide me with a loving home life.

"Until that is, my father, and I do regard him as my real father, suddenly died. Then again, she had to make tough choices and compromises to have happiness and fulfillment, but keep me in a safe and stable home, albeit one without her. That was hard for her, I realize that now.

"For decades I walked around with that angry little boy inside me, who felt abandoned and unloved, he's gone now and I'm finally free of him. But I let that little boy take it out on her when she was dying, to my eternal regret; I denied her the love I felt she denied me. I was wrong, I always had her love, but didn't understand her, so I judged her and hurt her instead.

"I don't want to undo what she and my father did to save their marriage and raise me properly. Telling Assunta, a frail old man at the end of his life that he had a son would help no one; it would be cruel. Better to let him rest in peace."

Jesse looked down at the table, then at her dad, she was quiet for a time that seemed much longer than it was, then nodding her head, she finally spoke, "I think I see where you're coming from dad, I'm glad you've finally resolved the issue with your mom. I would like to have known Viviana, more about her anyway. Can I have some of the pictures of her? Maybe we can visit her grave sometime and bring flowers. I'd like us to do that."

"I'd like to do that too. It's about time, and yes we should put some of these pictures around, that is after my party." Nick grinned.

"Well Nick, I'm sorry the surprise element is gone, but I think we've had enough surprises. Actually, I'm a little relieved you know about it. I was worried that you'd be angry with me for doing it against your wishes, grumpy!" laughed Lidia, ruffling her husband's hair.

'Nah, I'm okay with it. In fact, better than okay, ecstatic, that two such lovely women and dear friends want to go to all this trouble just to celebrate me. I'm blessed." He leaned over and gave them both a peck on the cheek.

"Oh dad, mom just wanted an excuse to throw a party," Jesse said, grinning slyly at her mother.

"Jesse!" Lidia was indignant.

"Oh, Mrs. Dalloway, you know you can't help yourself." Nick laughed. Then he went silent, contemplating if this was the right time to unburden himself. He decided it was. "Lidia, you're not the only one who was keeping a secret, I have one too."

"Oh? Do you mean surprise or secret?" Lidia asked, looking from Jesse to Nick, her feeling of gaiety, suddenly ebbing away.

"Secret, and worse, a lie. The urologist didn't just send me away with some exercises, diet and lifestyle advice, he wants to perform a biopsy in two weeks because my prostate is quite enlarged and my p.s.a. is still elevated," Nick said, swallowing hard watching his wife's face for the reaction he knew was coming.

But Jesse spoke first. "Oh, dad!" she cried, bringing her hands to her face.

Lidia shouted, "I don't believe this, Nick. Why do you think you need to lie to me and hide something that first, I should know, and second, I will find out anyway? What were you thinking, you idiot!"

"Mom!" Jesse cut in.

"She's right, Jess. Lidia, I wasn't thinking, not about me, but about you. Don't you think I know how much you care and worry about everyone in this family. I just didn't want to upset you. Forgive me, please?" he said, reaching-out for her hand. "I need your support now, not your anger," Nick said, looking contrite.

Lidia took a deep breath, and exhaling loudly, said, "Okay, I can forgive you, I guess. But I'm still really mad. I'll support you all the way, but from now on Nick, we see the specialist together, agreed?"

Agreed," said a relieved Nick.

Hubbard squashed

BECKY STRETCHED HER long, black-nylon clad legs

awkwardly over the maze of packing boxes strewn about the apartment, searching for her new bejeweled, black satin stiletto sling backs. *Aah, there you are,* she thought triumphantly, raising the pair in one hand above her head, whilst hopping over to the new ottoman-cum-coffee table, where she settled to strap them on.

As she secured the final buckle and stood to admire her new purchase, her cell phone rang. Rushing to the desk, she found it buried amidst an array of various files, receipts and 'urgent' mail.

The caller was her eldest daughter. "Okay, Kate I'll be right there. Just try to humor him, but whatever you do, don't let him get in that car!"

Oh Christ! I just knew he'd pull something like this! But today, of all days, Nick's birthday party, god, I just hope I can keep a lid on him …thought Becky, frantically pulling-on her coat, grabbing her purse and car keys. Slamming the apartment door closed, she skidded on the tiled hallway towards the elevator for the underground parking. Finally, after pounding the down button in frustration for what seemed an eternity, the elevator doors opened.

I should warn Lidia, what'll she think? she's worked so hard to make this special…

"Hi, Lidia, listen I've got a bit of a crisis…what?

No, we're still coming, although you may wish we weren't, Paul's pissed, apparently been drinking since he got home after helping out. Kate's with him, I don't want him to drive, but if he insists on coming to the party, I'll have to bring him with me. Please alert the guys and make sure whatever he drinks is watered-down, okay? But I'll do my best to have him stay put and sleep it off."

"Oh great, how long ago did he leave, Kate?" Becky was at a red light now and risked answering her phone, seeing the call was from her daughter.

"The cab picked him up just two minutes ago, I'm sorry mom, he must've overheard me talking to you and guessed what was up," said a distraught Kate.

"Never mind, it's not your fault, you shouldn't have to deal with something like this and I promise you, it WON'T happen again!"

"Anyway mom, it's more his foul mood I'm worried about than the actual amount he's drank."

"Thanks love. Don't worry, I'll take it from here."

Javi's penthouse suite throbbed with a cacophony of elated voices and the clink of glasses, above which wailed the saucy falsetto of Shirley & Company's, *Shame, Shame, Shame!* The elevator opened on to the columned marble foyer.

Well, the party seems to be in full swing, no awk-

ward silence, so Paul must be behaving himself, thank God. Well, here goes! thought a resolute Becky stepping forward, tossing her coat to the hired butler. She patted her hair in place, pulled-up her bra strap and strode straight into the fray.

"Hi handsome, Happy Birthday!" Becky beamed with false bravado as she kissed Nick on both cheeks and gave him a warm hug, then immediately turned to Lidia who was at his side, "Where is he? Is he okay?"

"He's not too bad, a little snarky, won't take any food, but wants to keep drinking. He's over there at the kitchen island with the guys and Voula. She's brought her tarot cards and is doing mini readings for fun. She's good, quite fascinating actually."

"Thanks Lid, I think I'll head over there and shadow him, just to make sure he doesn't escalate."

"May I, madam?" Nick proffered his arm, offering to escort his anxious friend through the labyrinth of dancing and drinking partiers to the other side of the expansive room, where her very surly and drunk husband stood slightly swaying.

"Okay, is there anyone else who has a question for Spirit? Anyone who needs to know a secret, uncover a mystery perhaps?" Voula teased good naturedly, as she cleansed and reshuffled her well-worn Thoth Tarot deck.

The sudden feel of Becky's hand on Paul's shoulder, the sense of her magnetic presence, provoked him to speak, "Yeah, I have a mystery I'd like your 'Spirit' to solve for me," Paul sneered, his desperate blood-shot eyes at once challenging and imploring Voula, who met his gaze with compassion.

"Of course, Paul. What is the answer you seek?" she responded in a low, calm voice, slowly shuffling the cards as she did so, as Javi, Frank, Jesse, Becky, and Nick waited, tense with anticipation.

"I want to know…who's… been fucking…my wife," he challenged, leaning over the island, grinning menacingly.

"Hey, now that's no way…,"

Frank didn't get to finish his sentence as Paul pushed him off and repeated his belligerent request, even louder now, gripping the edge of the island, the veins in his muscular forearms pulsing, he yelled, "WHO'S BEEN FUCKING MY WIFE?"

Voula pulled herself up. "Okay, just calm down, now. I'll draw a card, only if you calm down." Seeing him relax his grip and stand back, she threw the card, "Aah haa! The Knight of Wands… *reversed*!" she exclaimed.

Just then Paul caught Javi's eyes quickly avert; it was in that instant he knew; Paul just knew what he had felt all along, "Why you bastard, you fucking suave, smooth-talking, full-of-yourself bastard!"

Paul picked-up a small, round squash from the harvest basket at his elbow and flung it hard and fast toward Javi. It sounded a loud thump as it made contact with flesh and bone, sending Nick Ponti reeling backwards, banging his head against the refrigerator's stainless-steel door, where he slid, senseless, to the floor.

The group stood in stunned silence for a second, then crowded in on the immobile figure.

"Oh, my god! Dad? Daddy!" a frantic Jesse shrieked as she leant over her father. Lifting his eyelids, seeing his eyes lolling in their sockets, she cried, "Get an ambulance, NOW!"

"It's coming, Jess, I just called, stay calm." Josh soothed Jesse, as he put his arm around her shoulder and pulled her to his chest.

Voula and Lidia were kneeling beside Nick now, taking his pulse, tapping his face and calling his name, trying to get a response, when his eyelids twitched and he groaned, "Oh Christ! What happened?"

IL ZUCCONE

"So, you were clobbered by a winter squash, eh? I guess from now on we should call you 'il zuccone', the pumpkin head, after Donatello's famous statue," chuckled Franco Lombardo, Assistant Head of Italian Studies, who listened to Nick's tale with more than slight schadenfreude, a large glass of Merlot perched upon the convenient shelf of his rotund belly.

"Wow, now that's a real birthday bash!" shouted a voice from the bar.

"What kind was it, Nick?" asked Karl Jorgen, professor of Physics.

"Does it really matter?" an exasperated Nick sighed, still sporting a puffy, bruised visage.

"Of course, it matters, the subtle nuances amongst your various winter squashes in terms of their ratio of mass to aerodynamic efficiency and ultimate force as projectile missiles cannot be underestimated here."

"Piss-off," grunted Nick who was fed-up with the ribbing his 'bashing' inspired, which was a diversion from the self-serving whining and sycophantic strategizing typical of their quarterly college drinks party; the assembled feasting upon this bird with good-humored relish…for a change.

"Oh, I agree!" joined Jorgen's colleague, "If it was, say a tender Delicata we are not very impressed, but an injury sustained by the assault of a sturdy Acorn, well then, I think a Vic Cross might not be out of order?"

"Or if our stalwart Nicholas had survived a brutal clubbing with a Butternut, now there's heroics!" added Professor Glen Davies of Modern Literature, whom Nick always thought a 'smug twit'.

"Oh, alright! It was a Hubbard, if you must know. Satisfied? Now shut-up and somebody get me a drink."

Nick's ill humor owed less to his colleagues' teasing than it did to his resentment of Javi's disappearing when the 'squash hit the fan', leaving Nick to do clean-up, acting as peacemaker, Javi being as ever, all cock and no balls. *Well, he'd better show for Frank's 'truth and reconciliation' or I'll find him and give him a good bashing myself. Anyway, I owe him one,* Nick grumbled morosely into his glass.

The incident made Nick ruminate on the relationship between Paul and Javi, realizing that it had always been a rivalrous one from the beginning. Paul was an out-going, handsome boy whose good looks and guileless charm was popular with all ages and ranks of the female species, from his older sisters to his teachers and of course, peers.

Javi, on the other hand was a gangly, pimply, shy kid who stammered through a set of gunky metal braces, he was taller than most of the class, but hadn't yet filled-out, earning him the nickname 'string-bean'.

Nick now realized that Javi's jealousy of Paul emerged in sly acts of passive-aggression, telling lies about, or to whomever, Paul was dating or had his eye on at the moment, just to wind him up and watch the famous Deauville temper explode all over some unsuspecting girl, or get him in a tussle with a rival.

Javi, being 'a quick study' would offer to help Paul with difficult homework assignments, then lead him astray, sabotaging his already slim chance of passing.

But by sixteen, Nick recalled, the tables suddenly turned; Javi filled-out and proved to be an able athlete, his skin cleared, his stammer finally remediated. Nick saw him blossom as his older brothers fled the nest, making Javi, Imelda's 'man about the house' when his father was away on business, which was often.

This was a role Javi relished, it made him feel mature and important. He learned the art of charm as well; whereas Paul had a boyish, natural charm, Javi's was sophisticated, cultivated, and focused. He never seemed to do anything without a view to his own benefit, a trait that Nick found a little too mercenary, especially when it came to girls; once Javi discovered the joys and power of his sexuality, he used and exerted it fiercely.

However, like the proverbial rake, the progress Javi made through the female population blazed a lonely trail to an ultimately pointless and empty destination. *And just look what he's done now, ruined his friendships and a marriage,* Nick sighed, as he swallowed the last few drops of scotch, which instead of making him feel better, suddenly made him very sad.

LES MISERABLES

NICK'S TURNING FIFTY may have advanced his life's journey, but it felt like fate was turning the tide against him. If the 'birthday bashing' and his friends' betrayal, fractured friendships, and broken marriage, weren't enough, when Nick wearily crossed the threshold of his home, passing he hoped, from the cares of the world to the peace of his hearth and the succor of his table, Lidia greeted him with unwelcome news:

"Why are you so late? We have to be there in a little more than an hour, you barely have time to freshen-up and eat. I'll warm some soup for you, while you go up and get changed."

"Changed? Changed for what?" cried Nick, dumping his briefcase on the bench.

"For the musical? Les Miserable? Remember, I reminded you on Monday. Sheesh," exclaimed an exasperated Lidia as she bustled into the living room, Nick following, more annoyed now than perplexed.

"And *I* told *you,* that I hate musicals and didn't want to go! Couldn't you have taken Becky or Siobhan instead?"

"No Nick, because I didn't want you to seem a rude ingrate to one of my best friends and his partner who bought the tickets for *your* birthday. And, Shelton and Clive are going that night, they're seated beside us, so lighten up. It won't be that bad, I hear it's got good reviews," said Lidia a little too brightly.

"Oh yeah? From who? Idiots who like musicals, that's who, the dimwits who know nothing about theatre and even less about French revolutionary history, never mind literature!" Nick's color was flushed now, a signal that he was working-up to one of his rants.

"I hate the shallow characterizations and even

crappier stagecraft, which consists chiefly of the 'actors' strolling aimlessly around, except when they aren't pompously posturing, or stomping down stage, planting themselves heroically, legs spread, chest thrust, before the incredulous audience waiting in breathless anticipation for the next ludicrous declaration meant to advance the thin, inane plot." Nick was in full indignation now and stood resolute in the middle of the living room, giving his comic impression of heroic acting.

"What about the music? You like music, and opera, don't you?" offered Lidia, in a feeble attempt at placation.

"Buy the c.d., download it to your iPod, just ditch the amateur dramatics."

"But there's the dancing, Nick, you like dance."

"Dear god, the humanity!" Nick clasped his forehead and dropped on to the couch.

"Oh, talk about amateur dramatics." Lidia shook her head in disgust.

An hour later, an excited Lidia settled-in to the seat beside her resigned, but still disgruntled husband just in time for the lights to dim and the musical to begin.

She turned to smile at Nick and squeeze his hand, when he moaned, "Oh why, in God's name, am I here?"

Lidia, unperturbed, whispered, "Shush, now's not the time for an existentialist debate Nick, just watch the show."

Finally, after what seemed to Nick a hellish eternity, the lights went-up and it was intermission. He and Shelton found themselves elbow to elbow at the front of the bar, Shelton being as disgruntled as Nick on account of also being there on sufferance, his partner Clive, being as enthusiastic a musicals fan as Lidia.

"So, Shelton, tell me, what do you think of it so far?" Nick asked.

"Quite surprising," responded Shelton. "I mean, I had no idea that the title referred as much to the quality of the drama as it does to the audience suffering its protracted spectacle."

"Oh, don't I know it!" Nick exclaimed, glad to have found a kindred spirit. "I was tempted during the second act, when Jean Val Jean was yet again eluding his captors, to cry-out, "Look! *Over there*! He's in the tunnel! Just to get the damn thing over with. Anyway, I'll bet most of the audience believes this play is about the French Revolution!"

"Isn't it?" asked Shelton.

"No, Hugo wrote this about the 1832 Insurgent Barricade, when King Louis-Philippe was installed as monarch, that's forty-three years after the 'Reign of

Terror'!"

"Really? By the way, why are all the French kings called 'Louis'?"

"Because the French lack imagination?" Nick snickered.

Shelton laughed, ordered them two brandies, "And make them doubles."

Chapter Five

WINTER

THE CHAMOMILE CURE

THREE WEEKS LATER, Father Frank was bustling around the rectory's kitchen preparing for his 'truth and reconciliation' session with Nick, Javi and Paul. Even though he had conducted preparatory interviews with each separately, he still fretted silently to himself about the outcome, as he stowed the freshly baked cinnamon buns in the warming oven.

They were his antidote to discord, believing that what homemade cinnamon buns can't cure, there's no cure for. He reasoned that if it went well, then out they'd come, along with the Irish coffees. But, if things were discordant, or unresolved, there'd be no appetite for lingering over a sumptuous, homey treat, which he feared might be the outcome of this matter. Still, he liked having them handy as a 'consolation tool' in his reconciliation arsenal.

As it was, he prepared for a round of soothing

chamomile tea, it struck just the right chord for the enterprise of reconciliation and avoided the awkward asking how each wanted their coffee, he knew that it was usually black, but these were different and difficult times for his friends, which may have raised sugar, or dairy cravings, and the stimulation of caffeine was definitely something to be avoided.

In the end, he thought it best to settle for the pacifying pot of chamomile, passed around so each could begin the reconciliation process with the symbolic gesture of 'pouring-out' to each other.

As he was putting out the cups and saucers, Nick rapped loudly on the back door, "Invado!" answered Frank, with the Latin bid to enter.

"Ooh! It's a cold one out today, Frank!" said Nick, as he entered, energetically rubbing his cold hands together, his face burrowed into a long, winding scarf.

"So, close the door you lummox, that draft's brutal," commanded Frank. "And when you've got your coat and hat off, you can bring two more chairs in from the sitting room."

"Yes, sir! God, I'll bet Bishop Tutu never treated his underlings like this," laughed Nick, as he did the priest's bidding. "Is that alright, your worship?" Nick said as he arranged the chairs around the table.

"Oh no, it's all wrong. Too hierarchical. Damn,

now I wish I hadn't ditched the round table to make room for my rectory one. If I sit at the head, thus. I seem like a stern schoolmaster, ready to mete out a punishment, but if I don't and sit beside either Paul or Javi, it looks like I'm taking sides," Frank moaned.

"Yeah, I see what you mean," said Nick, rubbing his chin in contemplation. "Look, how 'bout we take the center leaf out to make it all cozy and collegial, then you and I sit at either end, not too far to seem hierarchical, but still in control, then Javi and Paul sit facing each other?" offered Nick.

"Oh, I guess so…but still that seems a bit confrontational," Frank sighed. "Uh!… It's the best we can do I suppose." With that, both men set about removing the center-leaf and re-arranging the seating.

When Nick opened the kitchen door to take out the compost bucket, he was surprised to see Javi, arrived suspiciously early, but arrived nonetheless, standing on the stoop, about to knock. "Well stranger, glad to see you actually made it," greeted Nick.

"What, you didn't think I'd come?" challenged Javi, as Nick pushed past him on his way to the compost pile. Hearing no response, Javi, shaking his head, made his way to the kitchen, where he greeted Frank who was preparing to brew the tea. He carefully draped his bespoke camel hair coat and paisley cashmere scarf around the back of the chair that Frank directed him to occupy.

There he sat, hands folded in front of him, watching his friends in silence, waiting for the drama to unfold. He didn't have to wait long, as a few minutes later a somber and sober Paul took his chair, without removing his down jacket, he hunkered down facing Javi and glowered.

After the ritual pouring of the tea and Frank's establishing of the gathering's purpose and its ground rules; the purpose being understanding, hopefully leading to forgiveness. The rules were: no speaking out of turn, swearing, judging, shouting or violence of any kind, just accept each other's truth. Keep it cool, calm and compassionate, was his mantra to them.

After Paul made a sincere and humble apology to Nick for the squash incident and ruining his birthday party, he made a grudging acknowledgment to Javi that a drunken assault wasn't the best way to express his feelings.

All things and Paul's mood considered, this was the best Frank could hope for. It was clear he wasn't going to expose the depth of his feelings about Becky and Javi's betrayal, so Frank turned to Javi.

"I know I deserve your anger, Paul. But I want

you to understand that I didn't set out to seduce Becky, even though I'd admired her for a very long time. Our attraction was mutual and only developed into an affair when Becky made it clear that she was unhappy in her marriage. We were working closely on a few projects of mine and we just responded to our feelings for each other."

Paul's shoulders slackened and he sat back in his chair, listening with intent as Javi went on.

"To tell the truth, she was lonely, I guess. She felt misunderstood and said she couldn't talk about her feelings openly and honestly with you."

It was then that the flint struck a spark, Paul jumped-up, chin jutting out, and yelled, "What the fuck do you know about my marriage? Eh? Just some wine-soaked pillow talk, you creep!

"Becky could talk to me, I begged her to talk to me," he cried out, pounding his fist against his chest. "But no, I'm too thick, I guess. She'd rather talk rubbish to *you*, she ran to *you*, when she had *me*, heart, and soul. You know what, Javi? The only thing that's stopping us from being friends again is that I hate your fucking guts!" Frank moved to Paul's side, put his arm firmly around his shoulders and felt him heave a great sob.

Nick stood by on high alert, when Javi, his passion roused, stood and yelled back, "Oh yeah! Well, I can't understand that, as we have so much in common, being members of the exclusive club called, 'Men Becky Used to Love'," he said with contempt.

Nick pushed his arm firmly across Javi's chest, prompting him to sit down, which he did. Frank steered an emotional Paul away from the table toward the living room, where he tried to get him to sit down, but Paul refused. "Why should I sit down? Or calm down? Anyway, what do you know about adultery? You're not even married for chrissake. This is a farce… I'm going home."

"Please Paul, I can't let you go like this. Look at the state of you, face livid, eyes swollen, let me get you a cool cloth for your face, then you can sit quietly and gather yourself together," offered Frank, in his best ministerial manner.

Paul walked over to the mirror, "Good God! my eyes are redder than a Sudbury sunset! What was in that tea you gave us?"

"Why nothing, it's only chamomile."

"Chamomile! Why didn't you say, you dimwit? I'm allergic to chamomile! That's it, I'm outta' here, while I'm still alive." Paul left, slamming the front door on his anxious, well-meaning friend.

Frank shot back to the kitchen, wringing his hands in despair, only to find that Javi was making for the back door, Nick following close behind, advising, "Just stop there for a minute, will you? Give the guy a chance to escape with some dignity."

Javi released the doorknob, exhaled loudly and turned to face Nick, "Alright, I've had enough conflict for one day. So, what say we count down…one potato…two potato…," Javi sneered bitterly.

"God, you really can be a hateful bastard when you're cornered. You know Javi, this meeting was as much for your benefit as it was for Paul's."

"Ah well, no good deed goes unpunished, eh Nick?" Javi countered, not letting his defenses down.

"I know you don't believe that Javi," joined Frank. "But of course, if it makes you feel better you can choose not to face your guilt and forgive yourself, because that's who you're really angry with."

"Bullshit, Frank!" Javi shot back. "You know who I'm really angry with?… Becky. I wanted us to be together; openly as a couple… I loved her, I love her still and she me, but she's in denial, because of you and Paul and your guilt trip.

"The only thing that's going to make this right is to prove to you that we are in love. Becky and I belong together, and I'll get her back." With that, Javi yanked the door open and stomped out.

"Oh dear," Nick said wearily, lowering himself into his chair. "Cool, calm and compassionate, eh? Huh, how did you go from Desmond Tutu to Jerry Springer in under an hour, Frank? That's some gift you've got."

"Alright, ha, ha, ha! I misjudged the situation, okay? I guess, despite counseling they just weren't ready," replied a despondent Frank.

"Well, that's an understatement…but, do you really think he meant it? About getting Becky back?"

Frank sat across from his friend and contemplated the question for a moment. "I do think Javi is in love with Becky, so yes, he may try to get her back. As for Becky, I think Javi's the one in denial there, I don't think she'll go back to him, if anything, given time, she may return to Paul."

"Oh, and how do you know that?" asked Nick.

"It's classified," said Frank, with an air of finality.

The stresses of the morning suddenly made Nick crave something sweet and warm. "Uh, Frank…are those cinnamon buns I smell?"

"You okay, Nick?" Lidia asked, as they sat, anxiously, in the hospital's pre-op waiting room. She squeezed his hand and leaned toward him, the faint scent of her white bergamot, tingling his nostrils.

"I'm thirsty," Nick said, his tongue struggling to free itself from the paste of congealed saliva coating the inside of his mouth. His stomach grumbled, empty from its twelve-hour fast.

"You can have a nice hot cup of herbal tea when we get home. Okay?" Lidia said.

"Tea? After this biopsy ordeal, I'll need a nice big glass of Barolo," Nick responded.

"Well, I hope they can take you in soon. I hate these waiting rooms. And after the procedure, there'll be a lot less Barolo and Bolognese for you, mister. Steamed fish and steamed vegetables, the omega 3's in fatty fish and cruciform vegetables are excellent for prostate issues, as is a daily dose of flax oil. Becky told me when we discussed your biopsy, her brother had the same issue," Lidia said.

"Tell me Lidia, why do women have to share *everything*, down to the last gory detail?"

"It's just what we do, Nick. It's in our DNA to pass on information, especially about healing; we were the first healers and doctors after all."

"Ha! More like witch doctors," scoffed Nick, crossing his legs. "Okay doc, listen to this," he said, peering through his half-glasses at a pamphlet on endocrinology. "The human intestinal tract, upper and lower, is six meters or twenty feet long. Imagine that! No matter if you're a Pygmy or a Watusi, the same length of guts are stuffed inside you, neat as you like. God is certainly miraculous." He lowered the pamphlet and mused.

"Well, that just goes to prove that the supreme deity is female," exclaimed Lidia.

"Oh, and how's that?" challenged Nick.

"Oh, c'mon Nick, only a woman can pack like that," Lidia chuckled.

Well, sighed Nick to himself, *at least she's taking it all in good humor. My wonderful wife, I think I'll take her away in February, just the two of us on one of those Caribbean trips she keeps mentioning. Just have to get through the next two weeks 'til we get my results.*

THE RETURN TO work for both Nick and Lidia had the salutary effect of taking their minds off Nick's impending prognosis, during the day at least; Lidia's office was frantically busy with finalizing the next season's edition of *Your Best Life,* and the activity in Nick's college was that of marking term papers, preparing and scheduling end-of-semester exams. All were complicated by the confounding influences of Toronto's capricious winter weather, bringing outbreaks of colds and flu, which meant bouts of short staffing on both fronts.

Even the indomitable Shelton, who annually boasted, with a little conceit, that he never gets sick, got very sick, leaving Lidia with several of his engagements to either cancel, find a pinch-hitter or be a sub herself. Being called upon in his absence, to be a guest speaker at the annual Taste Canada Awards Gala, while fulfilling her other promotional media commitments.

None the less, amidst all the frantic November, pre-Christmas activity, there were quiet moments, moments of doubt and fear, the dark nights of the soul which afflicted them both. Leaving the marital bed to wander the house, feeling the daggers of worry in his back, Nick made silent pilgrimages downstairs to the kitchen.

He opened the refrigerator door, stood somnambulant in its eerie, lonesome glow, then finding no appeal of comfort in its cold offerings, retreated wearily back to bed. Lying rigid beside his silent wife, he stared worriedly at the ceiling until dawn aroused his need for slumber.

This ritual repeated itself several times during the next two weeks, while Lidia's anxiety was manifest in her sporadic nocturnal wanderings, not to the fridge, but focused on the various common drawers and cupboards her family shared and cluttered.

Now the siren call of their wanton disarray lured her at all hours down to the kitchen, hallway, and laundry room to root out the dross, clear away the confusion, so all was orderly, tidy, manageable, beneath her control.

Satisfied with her covert nocturnal purging and cleansing, Lidia mounted the stairs quietly, gingerly sliding between the sheets beside her husband, to stare out the window until the rude morning sun blazed-up from the horizon, commanding her weary body to rise.

TWO WEEKS ELAPSED, finding Nick and Lidia aimlessly thumbing through back issues of Canadian Business and Vanity Fair in the urologist's half-empty waiting room.

Lidia took stealthy note of the other patients' demeanor, their body language going into and emerging from their consultations. She wondered which ones had gotten bad news, which one's reprieve? It was, to her surprise, difficult to tell either way, as most looked fairly weary, and grim, coming and going. Perhaps it was because it was late on a cold, drizzling Wednesday evening when everyone was just tired and wanted to be somewhere, anywhere, else.

Although Nick seemed engrossed in reading yet another profile of a smug C.E.O. of a banal, but lucrative stuffed-shirt corporation, his mind was in another zone, one that fantasy protected from paralyzing fear; he imagined himself parasailing far above a sun-spangled azure sea, drifting weightless above all the petty chaos of reality, just on and on, a warm gentle zephyr carrying him into the endless horizon.

"Mr. Ponti," the receptionist suddenly alerted them, "Dr. Hamra will see you now, first door on your left." Nick shot-up quickly, then uncharacteristically, strode briskly ahead of his wife, whose presence he suddenly seemed to have forgotten.

As Lidia managed to crowd-in next to her husband, shoulder to shoulder in the cramped, airless office, the doctor reviewed his notes, then addressed Nick over his half-glasses, "Mr. Ponti, I am pleased to inform you that the results of your biopsy are negative.

"Nevertheless, your condition needs monitoring and if it doesn't improve with the lifestyle changes I've recommended, such as weight loss, reducing your alcohol consumption, increasing your green vegetable intake, daily supplements of flax oil and daily vigorous exercise, we may consider if you need a transurethral reduction procedure, which is essentially scraping of the interior of the prostate to reduce its size."

The surgeon fixed his patient with a steely gaze, making Nick shift uneasily in his seat.

"Um well, yes that is good news…phew! I'll certainly continue with the regime you've prescribed, Dr. Hamra. God knows I don't want any more surgery…er, not that my experience at your capable hands was in any way…," Nick faltered, and Lidia interjected:

"What my husband means, doctor, is that he, with my support of course, will do all that is necessary to ensure his well-being. Isn't that so, Nick?" Lidia asserted, kicking her reticent, tongue-tied husband on the ankle.

"Oh, yes, yes…sure, just as Lidia says, with her support." Then coughing dryly, Nick continued, "I'll certainly make progress towards better health. Now, is that it? Can we go…um, see we have a little shihtzu that needs walking."

"Of course, Mr. Ponti, Mrs. Ponti. I'll see you, Mr. Ponti, in three months," Dr. Hamra concluded, with a worried expression and a little chagrin at his patient's hasty retreat.

"A shihtzu that needs walking? What, are you nuts? Dr. Hamra must think you're, no, WE – are idiots, caring more about our fictional dog's urinary functions, than we care about yours! You're insane!" Lidia fumed as she walked briskly beside her indifferent husband, heading towards their car.

"You know, maybe we should get a dog," Nick pondered, as he turned-on the ignition.

"Why? What on earth for?" scoffed Lidia, as she buckled herself in.

"Because it would motivate me to walk more, you know, if I had a nice dog to walk," Nick reasoned.

"Or you could just start using the gym facilities and pool at the university available to you for free, right at your workplace, what could be more convenient than that!" Lidia retorted loudly.

"The pool? I abhor the smell of chlorine and hate getting wet in the winter, and the gym just makes me sweaty, then I have to shower all over again, which I've already done once that day and that's enough getting wet for me."

"Okay then, try easing into a more active lifestyle, get off the subway a few stops early and walk the rest of the way, take the stairs at work instead of the elevator," Lidia countered calmly, barely able to contain her frustration.

"That just makes me hungrier, so I'll want to eat more when I get home," argued Nick as he pulled into their parking pad.

"Ach! I give up," Lidia said, releasing her seatbelt.

"I still think I should get a dog," Nick refrained.

"Oh, for the love of god!" Lidia shouted, stomping angrily up the stairs into the house.

The kitchen table was set for three, the comforting smell of osso bucco infused the air. Jesse stood at the cook-top ready to start the risotto; risotto Milanese and osso bucco being her newly mastered culinary feats, dishes acquired under the tutelage of her father.

Jesse's recent interest in cooking was motivated as much by Josh's culinary acumen, as the necessity for economy, as when it was her turn to provide a meal, she inevitably resorted to some greasy overpriced Thai take-out, the charm of which was wearing thin, especially since Josh was quite accomplished in Asian cuisine. They were saving for their mini-Cooper, European summer tour, and so were pinching pennies.

"Well, how'd it go?" Jesse asked apprehensively, as she turned to look at her parents.

"Fine sweetie, it's all good. The results were negative," Nick assured her, heading to the hallway to hang up his coat.

"Oh, thank god!" Jesse exclaimed, rushing to give her father a hug. "I'm so glad. So, everything's fine, right? You aren't just saying that?"

"No! I'm fine, really, the patient's gonna be here for a long time yet. And to prove it, I even bought green bananas!" He handed her a bunch from his string bag.

"Oh dad," Jesse laughed, heading back to the kitchen.

Nick peeked into the saucepan of simmering rice. "Mm, looks and smells great Jess, I'm starving."

"It won't be long now, and no, I didn't forget to put in a good pinch of coriander," she said proudly, stirring the pot. "And like you taught me, never rush risotto. So, go open some wine while we wait."

Nick went to their custom-fitted enoteca in the back porch and chose a 2013 Chianti Classico, an excellent vintage, one he'd been saving for a special occasion.

"I'm so glad he's got a clean bill of health, mom. You must be so relieved," Jesse said.

"Well, not quite. It seems your father still has a long way to go in his commitment to improved health, like starting regular exercise," Lidia sighed.

"Dad," Jesse said, as her father opened the wine, "mom tells me you have to start an exercise program, I'd be happy to show you some yoga moves."

"No!" Nick responded a little too loudly and quickly, startling his daughter. "Um, no thanks Jess, I just can't see myself in yoga pants. I'll figure something out… soon…don't you worry. In the meantime, let's have a nice quite dinner." He handed his daughter and wife a glass of wine.

After taking a sip of wine, Lidia said firmly and levelly, "Just remember Nick, no dog!"

CAFFÈ CORRETTO CONDOLENCE

BRRRING, BRRRING, BRRRING, the vintage doorbell sounded insistently, as Cheech impatiently cranked its ancient mechanism over and over.

"Cheech!" exclaimed a disheveled Nick, answering the door in his robe and slippers. "It's a bit early for you to be picking-up Aldo, isn't it?"

"Oh no, sorry son, it's Assunta…," whispered the distraught figure standing awkwardly on the stoop.

"You think you're Assunta?" Nick grimaced; the faint suspicion of dementia flicked across his mind.

"No, of course I don't. Do you think I'm nuts or

something? It's your dad, *he's dead!*" Cheech blurted out, now with more exasperation than the reverence he originally intended.

"Oh…oh… I'm so sorry, Cheech, please come in… I'll put some coffee on." Nick shuffled down the hall towards the kitchen, Cheech in tow.

Aldo appeared in his doorway; "Eh? That you Cheech? What the hell's going on? It's six in the a.m. for God's sake!"

Cheech stopped to deliver his news once again, this time with the downcast eyes and lowered voice that social convention required in such sensitive situations.

The two older men sat facing each other as Nick poured-out the dark, foaming espresso into three small ceramic cups.

"Uh Nick, can mine have a corretto?" Cheech indicated the addition of a splash of grappa to 'correct' the brew.

"Well, since you're pouring Nick, I'll have a corretto too, thanks," said Aldo.

"Oh, what the hell, I might as well have one too." Nick twisted the stopper from the best bottle of grappa he kept in the cupboard above the cups expressly for the purpose.

Nick sat down in the armchair at the head of the old pine table, a perch usually reserved for Aldo, but which in this unusual circumstance, he tacitly relinquished to his bereaved son-in-law.

"Well Cheech, what happened? I mean, the last time I saw him, just a week ago, he seemed to be much better, color in his cheeks, improved appetite, and energy. He was in good spirits."

"I know Nick. But it's not unusual for people with critical illness to suddenly rally just before their death, I know my Carmela did, and my dad likewise. It's as if they get a little 'last hurrah', to like, say good-bye to life and their loved ones," Cheech said thoughtfully, taking a sip of his hot coffee.

"Yeah, I heard of that," confirmed Aldo. "I remember great Uncle Ercole, he rallied six or seven times. We all rushed to the nursing home each time, then he'd come around stronger than before! He'd rub his legs and say, 'Once the legs go boy, it's the end!' Ha! Lived 'til he was ninety-eight.

"Thinking back on it though, it was probably just his way of getting us all together," Aldo said, draining his cup.

"Yeah…well, I guess, in the case of Assunta, that is, my father, that's that, eh?"

"Yes, I'm afraid so, Nick…now you probably need some time to yourself," declared Cheech, rising. "I'll let you know about the funeral arrangements, thanks for the coffee. And my deepest condolences, son," he said, patting Nick on the arm as he passed him, on the way to the front door.

"Oh, god. That's the last thing I want to face. After my aunt and uncle died, I vowed never to attend another funeral...unless of course, it's my own," he moaned aloud, holding his bowed head between his hands.

"Oh, don't take it so hard, Nick. He was an old man who led a good and happy life. And just think how nice it was that you could get to know him before he died. He liked you a lot, thought you were good company, so *coraggio*!" said Aldo, placing his warm, reassuring hands on his son-in-law's shoulders.

THE WHEEL OF MISFORTUNE

MOST OF THE residents attended the memorial mass in the chapel on the grounds of the retirement home. They then assembled outside, near the river, for the scattering of Assunta's ashes, after which there was to be coffee and sandwiches in the lounge.

The day was brisk, breezy, and bright. Aldo and Cheech stood out of ear shot from the rest, taking stock of the residents.

"Geeze, Aldo, just look at some of these geezers, I'm not sure whether we should help them in, or dig them in!"

"I know," whispered Aldo. "Look at that one with the oxygen tank, 'The Wheezer', emphysema, without a doubt. And look at the color on his friend, the one who always scarfs four cream doughnuts at tea break, 'Mr. Sweet Tooth', bound to have hypertension and type-2 diabetes."

"Yeah, and this one in the wheelchair, with the inhaler, 'Ol' Ironsides'," Cheech said, nudging his friend he added, "fibrillations and asthma, to say nothing of the 'Old Shuffler' with the walker, congestive heart failure, bet you anything!"

"Baloney! You watch too much Dr. Oz, you can't tell congestive heart failure from here," challenged Aldo.

"Bet I can. Bet I can give odds on how long he's probably got left too!" said Cheech triumphantly.

"You're on," Aldo's eyes lit up. "And what about the others, wise guy? Care to make a little book on them?"

"Absolutely," Cheech laughed. "Hey, Aldo, you think the guys at the club might want a piece of this action?"

"I don't see why not," Aldo concurred.

Cheech was thoughtful for a moment then addressed his friend, saying, "You don't think that, well, that it's wrong in some way do you, Aldo?"

"What wrong? We're not popping them off or hastening their demise, just looking to make a little profit anticipating the Almighty's timetable," Aldo reasoned.

"Right, scheduling's not up to us. We'll send a nice wreath," said Cheech, feeling reassured now.

"Or a charitable donation. No one can say we're disrespectful," confirmed Aldo.

"No, of course not. We'll call it, The Wheel of Misfortune," declared Cheech, pleased with his pun.

"I like it! Heh, heh…The Wheel of Misfortune," Aldo said smiling, jingling the change in his pocket.

LIDIA STOOD QUIETLY by her husband, firmly holding his hand while his father's ashes were scattered, and the benedictions intoned. Nick was surprised at how little ash was produced from a body, as he watched it drift out over the river in a whitish-grey stream, dispersed by the four winds, out to the other side of the Humber's bank, across and beyond the meadow.

As Lidia turned to head for the lounge and the reception, she felt a tug on her arm, "Nick? What's wrong? Don't you want to go in?"

"Not just yet. I want to sit on that bench and smoke my cigar, if I may," Nick said quietly.

"'Course you may, just don't linger too long in this damp air, and get a chill, okay? Do you want me to sit with you?" asked Lidia, reaching-up to him, tucking a wayward lock of hair behind his ear.

"No, no. I'm fine; just want to be on my own for a bit. Go in and get some hot coffee, you must be freezing. I'll be along soon," he gave her hand a reassuring squeeze as she turned to walk away.

Nick sat quietly, elbows on knees, blowing smoke rings and contemplating the length of his cigar's ash, as he did so he thought:

Well, then I guess it's true, all we ultimately amount to is ashes, prince, or pauper, makes no difference in the end.

But do we all die denied the crucial truth about ourselves? About our lives. Is the truth somewhere between and not in the stories we tell, like my mom's, my dad's about how to balance the scales, to make them justify...

But which story is true? My mom's impetuous love for Assunta? My dad's possessive love of my mom? Betrayal... forgiveness...just a divine jest they never saw the inside of... wonder what mine will be...guess time will tell.

With that last thought he stubbed out his cigar against the bench's concrete frame, then rose to join his wife at the reception.

RAOUL: STIRRED THEN SHAKEN

LAKE ONTARIO'S NOVEMBER gales were raging against the city, pinging ice pellets on the Ponti's bedroom windows where Nick and his wife were snuggled-up, oblivious to the maelstrom without, ensconced in the downy warmth of their king-size sleigh bed.

While the ethereal jazz of Ahmad Jamal soothed the weather demon, Lidia eagerly leafed through brochures for Caribbean vacations Becky gave Nick to consider. He was propped-up with his usual two large pillows and another across his lap holding the latest edition of *Cucina Italiana* he intently perused for the next, best thing to do with the dread zucchini.

"Oh, just look at that Nick! How fabulous to charter our own little luxury cruiser to island-hop, docking at the ancient trading ports of the Caribbean, or dropping anchor off a deserted palm-treed island. Our own private oasis where we can swim naked, feast on grilled flying fish and reef lobster, mangoes, coconuts and papaya," she said, her eyes closed, reveling in the scene.

Nick dropped his magazine and glanced over at the glossy idyllic image his wife offered him. "Oh yeah, pass the sunscreen, please," he smiled.

Lidia rejoined, "And Raoul, pour me another martini and a rum punch for my friend, here."

"Raoul? Who's this Raoul?" Nick raised an eyebrow.

"Look, it's my fantasy Nick, if you want on board baby, there will be a Raoul!" Lidia laughed.

"C'mon Lidia, Raoul? Sounds like an oily Latin gigolo."

"Oh yeah, well Raoul, grab that jigger, I want service below deck, Mr. Ponti can serve himself!"

"Oh cara, that's so harsh… I know, why not give Raoul the evening off-let me serve you instead, eh…how about it?" he said stroking her shoulder.

"Mm, well okay," she purred, sliding down into the duvet, "Oh and Nick…I'd like it stirred please…then shaken".

A week later Nick, who was now in much improved spirits, decided to book a Caribbean mini vacation as a surprise for his wife and a second honeymoon for them both.

Athina, Picking-up the Pieces

Athina sat crossed-legged on Jesse's rug, towel-drying her long, honey-blonde hair, as Jesse made them coffee in her basement apartment's galley kitchen.

"So, what do you have on for today?" Jesse asked, carefully passing her a hot mug.

"I've got an appointment with an academic counselor at two-thirty at George Brown College," she said, her voice wavering slightly.

"Oh...um, do you want me to come with you? I mean just for moral support, no pressure though, if you'd rather go it alone," Jesse said inclining her head in a sympathetic gesture.

"I'm not sure. Well okay, if you don't have anything else on... look, I don't mean to seem ungrateful Jess," Athina reached for her friend's hand, "it's just that I really don't know anything anymore. Don't even ask me the time of day."

She looked pensive, then said, "Time though Jess, is just what I've got to figure out. I need to focus on my future, make it count this time. I'm twenty-two with no profession, partner, or place of my own…Look, what a mess I've made of my life." Distress suddenly deepened every line around her finely chiseled features.

"Look, you're have to take this one step at a time. See the counselor first, discuss their sommelier program, you might be surprised at how close you could soon come to getting your life back on a positive track. But you really need to settle things between you and Ainsworth," Jess said calmly and firmly.

"You're right, take it one step at a time, but it's hard not to panic. One minute I feel calm and think I know exactly what I want and am going to do, the next my guts are in a knot and I'm crying my eyes out, can't even get out of bed. I know I have to talk things out with Ainsworth, I still love him. But I just can't face him, I'm so ashamed," she began to tremble and then cry quietly, while her friend held her close.

IRIDESCENT BEADS OF steam covered the Ponti's kitchen window, a large Dutch oven and two casseroles waited on the warming tray should one of their guests want seconds. Lidia and Nick, back from their Caribbean adventure, still glowing with sun and contentment, passed around the majolica platters of bresaola, eggplant Parmigiano and polenta with mushroom ragù. Josh poured the wine.

When everyone was looked-after, Lidia turned to Athina enthusiastically. "It's so nice to see you, I often wondered how you were making-out in Montreal, such an exciting city. So, tell us what you've been up to."

"Well not much, that's exciting I mean. At first, I did work for Ainsworth, but that was mostly fetching, you know, being a general dogs' body, mostly I just felt in the way," she mumbled, addressing her plate, avoiding Lidia's gaze.

"Oh, sorry to hear that. Are you thinking of moving back for good then?" Lidia asked.

"Um, maybe, I'm just visiting for now. I did have a job in Montreal as hostess in a really popular bistro. The staff was passionate about what they were doing, the cuisine was innovative and local. And the wine cellar was extensive. Working there I became really interested in wine. But now, I just need a break, I'm a little homesick I guess," she smiled wanly.

"Of course, you must miss your family. I know Elena and Costas certainly missed you, even Dmitri does, I'll bet," laughed Nick.

"Well Nick, I appreciate the sentiment, but I'm

sure my little brother is happy to have his run of the house while mom and dad are in Corfu all month," Athina laughed.

"Yeah, that's a shame you won't see them this trip, Athina. Do they know you're back?" Josh asked.

"Uh, no, I haven't told them. Anyway, there's no point since I won't be seeing them."

Lidia caught a hint of something amiss and asked, "But, surely you've been to the house to see your brother, if only to keep an eye on what he's up to, for your parents I mean."

"No way, Dmitri would just think I'm trying to police him and his buddies, who when they're not at lectures, play X-Box until three a.m. and live on cola, beer, take-out pizza and souvlaki. If I showed-up they'd just expect me to clean-up."

"Ah, gotcha," Nick smiled broadly at Athina. "Anyway, we're glad to have our adopted daughter all to ourselves this time. Right, Lidia?"

"Of course, we are. Stay as long as you like, dear. You're always welcome here," assured Lidia.

"Thanks, you two. I really appreciate it. Do you mind if I don't finish my dinner, it tastes great, but I don't have much of an appetite at the moment, and I need to do a few things before I meet Kate at the movies," Athina said rising to take her plate to the counter.

"No, not at all, if I don't see you before you leave, have a good time and say hi to Kate for me," Lidia said.

"Will do," responded Athina descending the stairs, Josh calling after her, "Give you a lift in fifteen, ok?"

"Well ladies, gentleman, thanks for the wonderful food and company, I'll just help you clean-up, then I'll be off. Promised to relieve the last shift at The Dep," Josh said rising.

"Josh, just relax, finish your wine," invited Lidia.

"How're things going at the store? I keep meaning to drop by on my way home, but always manage to get side-tracked," Nick said.

"Business is great. I've got plans to bring-in some local artisan charcuterie, cheeses and gourmet flatbreads and some other quality snack foods, to give customers some choice. I can't lose the cheezies, chips and dips, but I can make a section within the coolers and two banks of shelves for better quality stuff, then see how it goes.

"Most of the producers I'm talking to require a fairly low minimum order from retailers, so I doubt I'll get stuck with the stuff. Anyway, if I do, there's always Jess here to feed, right?" he gave her a playful pinch on the cheek.

"You make that sound like it's a full-time job," she laughed.

"Well, it is!" Josh replied.

Jesse threw her napkin at him and he jumped-up, giving her a little kiss, "Athina'll be waiting in the car. Thanks again for the wonderful dinner, call you later Jess."

"Ciao!" said Nick and Lidia.

"Not going to the movies with Athina, Jess?" asked Nick.

"Not tonight dad, have to prepare for my seminar tomorrow and am still getting grief from power point. I'll just help mom clear-up, you go and put your feet-up, that was an awesome feast."

"My pleasure, and I'm glad you liked it, 'cause eggplant Parmigiano is your next lesson," declared Nick as he pushed back his chair, grateful of the opportunity to repair to the living room, put on a fire log, sink down into his wing chair and listen to some jazz.

As Jesse made to put the leftovers away, Lidia placed a hand on her arm. "Never mind that, Jess. Come, sit down and talk with me," she encouraged her daughter, sitting down at the half-cleared table, craning her neck to take a peek down the hallway, ensuring their confab, would not be overheard.

"What's-up, mom?" Jesse said, innocently.

"Well daughter mine, that's what I'd like to know. What's up with Athina? Why all the secrecy around her being back in town? She so glum, not like our serene goddess at all. No appetite and looks positively skeletal. So?" she said, raising her voice a notch, staring expectantly at her daughter.

"Oh! I just knew we couldn't put this past you. Why do you always 'notice' everything mom?" moaned Jesse.

"Why? Because it's my job. You'll understand once you're married and have a family of your own."

"Or, when the time comes to send you to a nursing home," teased Jesse.

"Don't try to obfuscate, young lady, back to the burning question," Lidia gave her daughter an arch look and folded her arms across her chest.

Jesse poured them each a little wine, "Mom, if I tell you, you understand I'll be breaking a huge promise to my best friend? So, you *have* to treat this with the utmost confidence, no exceptions, agreed?" Jesse implored.

"Agreed. Now spill," commanded a resolute Lidia.

"Well, I'm sure you've already guessed that Athina's in trouble."

"Oh god Jess, that's what I feared. Damn. Poor,

stupid girl! And what about Ainsworth? Won't he help her; step-up to the plate? I could cry, Jess, I really could just cry. That girl is like a daughter to me, and Elena and Costas are very dear friends. Sorry now that I asked. I guess I was hoping it was just an impetuous love affair gone wrong," Lidia said bitterly, taking a gulp of her wine.

"It is an impetuous affair gone wrong mom. Just not one between Athina and Ainsworth, because shortly after she got work at the bistro, Ainsworth broke-up with her over her relationship with Denis."

"Denis? Who's Denis?" Lidia asked, anxiously.

"Well, that's the problem, mom. He was Athina's boss. She and Denis had an affair, Athina got pregnant. Denis slapped her, pushed her around mom, told her to get rid of it, then fired her and cut-off contact.

"You see, his father-in-law bankrolls his bistros, so he wasn't interested in having the affair ruin his restaurant empire…the creep," Jesse said scornfully. "Anyway, the pregnancy issue was resolved, because Athina miscarried."

"Oh my god! She really has been through it," Lidia said, astonished.

Jesse continued, "Yes, and feels deeply ashamed and abused, and doesn't know which way to turn. But she's at least trying to get her professional life back on track, considering the sommelier course at George Brown College."

"Well, I really wish she'd talk to Elena, Athina needs her mother now," advised Lidia.

"Mom, what she needs now is us; Athina's worried that her parents will see this as proof that she can't manage her life. Remember the conflict over her dropping-out to follow Ainsworth to Montreal?"

"Oh yes, they were extremely upset," Lidia recalled.

"That's putting it mildly, mom. But yes, they'll be there for her, but only if she does what they think is best. She wants to make her own decisions."

"I understand. Athina's lucky to have a friend like you. How'd you get to be so wise, eh?" Lidia said, smiling at her daughter.

"Thanks mom, I like to think I get my smarts from you, you know Athina and I used to call you 'the laser'?"

They both laughed. Then Jesse seemed pensive, "There's one thing that's bugging me…I keep thinking about Athina and Ainsworth, and where I was with that issue just last year. I was the one feeling abandoned and abused. But now I have Josh, a great guy, and I'm happy. I never envisioned it would turn out so badly for Athina, yet so well for me." Jesse shook her head.

"Oh, now Jess, you can't take on the guilt for Athina's troubles. You're two different people, with two different destinies. You're with Josh because you chose to explore a relationship together. Athina chose her own path, but it's one that she can change if she chooses…it's up to her."

"I know mom, it's just that my life is so good right now, especially with Josh. Mom, I think he's 'the one'!" Jess said excitedly.

"Really? I'm so happy for you!" she gave her daughter a little hug. "Have you told him?"

"No, not yet."

"Best let him come to that realization on his own," Lidia advised.

"I'll just let things develop naturally."

"Good cara, that's the way, softly, softly," said Lidia.

THE METRO-SEXUAL QUIZ

IT WAS NINE-THIRTY on Friday morning as Nick stood in front of his bedroom mirror, vigorously rubbing a dab of cream into the crease of dry skin between his brows.

"Late lecture today?" asked Lidia emerging, bathrobed and fragrantly fresh from her shower.

"Yep, eleven-thirty," replied her husband, admiring her, feeling aroused, wondering if he had enough time for a little seduction.

"Hey, is that my forty dollar an ounce face cream you're slathering on your ugly mug?"

"What? You paid how much for this muck?" shouted Nick.

"Never you mind, how much. You can't put a price on beauty," said Lidia, snatching the jar from his hand and replacing the lid.

"Well, apparently you can-it appears it's worth forty dollars an ounce, by the way is that before or after tax?" asked Nick raising an eyebrow.

"Oh, ha ha. Just stay out of my cosmetics, okay? I mean what, you think you're a metro-sexual now?" laughed Lidia.

"I don't know, maybe. You know, I think I might qualify," said Nick, tucking-in his shirt, sucking-in his belly, pondering the possibility.

"Ok, then let's do the metro-sexual quiz, shall we?"

"Shoot," said Nick confidently.

"Do you use 'salon brand only' hair product?"

"Um, if shampoo qualifies as 'hair product', just what's on sale at the drug store."

"Then the answer is no. Next, what thread count

are our bed sheets?"

"What, how would I know? Who sits around counting the threads in their bed sheets?"

"Oh, no again. Mm, let's see, have you ever had a mani-pedi?"

"A mani what?... Well, I'm pretty open-minded, but I'd draw the line at any 'mani-pedi' action!"

"Uh…that's short for manicure and pedicure, Nick," said Lidia.

"Oh," said Nick.

"Sorry love, three strikes, you're out!" Lidia declared.

"Oh c'mon, I buy extravagantly expensive balsamic vinegar in sexy little bottles, trim my ear and nose hairs, even had my back waxed once, god that hurt! Doesn't that count for anything?" implored Nick.

"No, no and no," said Lidia with finality as she turned and sashayed away into her walk-in closet, laughing.

Later, as they walked arm in arm to the subway, Lidia asked Nick, "What do you think of Josh?"

"He's a nice, interesting guy, who treats my daughter well. So, what's not to like?" Nick responded casually.

"Good, because our daughter likes him a great deal," Lidia said, grinning.

"Oh, how great a deal are we talking about?" Nick looked down at his wife with interest.

"A great, big deal Nick, she's in love with him, she thinks he's 'the one'," she said lowering her voice.

"Oh, good," Nick whispered, mimicking his wife.

"So, since he might join the family, don't you think you'd better do some male-bonding with him?"

"Male-bonding? You read too much Cosmo, and anyway, what do you suggest as a 'male-bonding' activity? That we go out in the woods and kill something. Or no, let's have an arm-wrestle, go to a Monster Truck rally, drink beer until we both puke and cry, then get matching tattoos?" smirked Nick.

"No, and don't be so sarcastic. What about inviting him to join you, Paul and Frank at the Saturday market, involve him in preparing the dinner, he's quite a good cook."

"Well okay, that sounds alright, especially since we're down a man, now that Javi's licking his wounds in Montreal, shacked-up with a twenty-two-year-old lingerie model," said Nick glumly.

"He'll never change Nick, he's a swine where women are concerned. Becky was right to dump him," said Lidia in disgust.

"Hey, don't be so judgmental, that's one of my

best friends you're talking about. One that is as much sinned against as sinning…being collateral damage," said Nick sternly.

"Speaking of 'collateral damage' Nick, don't forget I'm meeting Becky for dinner tonight, we haven't had a chin wag for ages. I'm dying to find out how things are with her now that she's on her own."

"Well, give her my love and try not to be too late," Nick gave her a customary peck on the cheek and a cursory wave as they parted at the subway entrance, he going west, she heading east.

GOOEY CHEESE AND GIRL TALK

BECKY ARRIVED AT seven for dinner with Lidia at La Raclette, the trendy uptown place to eat, as its name suggested, hot, gooey cheese. It seemed seventies' fads like platform shoes, bohemian fashion and fondue were new again, only ironically so, according to the hipsters. Becky ordered a bottle of Saint-Emilion, then sitting back, savoring its silky, smoky vanilla finish, wondered what on earth could be ironic about fondue?

As it drew near seven-fifteen, growing impatient, Becky fidgeted with her cell phone, checking the messages before turning it off...no interruptions during dinner hour, which was her time. Then thinking of time, Becky turned her phone back on deciding to text Lidia, when she caught sight of her friend in the mirror opposite the banquette.

"Ah, there she is, at last!" Becky exclaimed, as Lidia shuffled in from the cold, shaking the new fallen snow from her silver puff-coat before handing it to the hostess.

After an exchange of warm busses, Lidia settled into opposite her friend. "Well, what a journey; the subway inexplicably halted service three stops from here, so thinking I needed the exercise, I decided to hoof it instead of waiting for the shuttle, then the snow flurry started! Couldn't call you, forgot to charge my phone before leaving the office...anyway, I've made it," she smiled at Becky as they raised their glasses.

After the waiter had taken their order of fondue with assorted crudités and croutons, Lidia appraised her friend, not having seen her for several months. "Love the new 'do', gold hi-lites are really pretty, and the layers, very fresh. Who'd you go to?" asked Lidia.

"Mimi at Sharif's did it; you know the new place in Yorkville?"

"Heard of it, haven't tried it, but I'll definitely book-in before Christmas. I'm so overdue for a new styling," she exclaimed as Becky topped them both up with more wine.

"How's Frank's book going? Have you two finished the photography?"

"We just wrapped it up last weekend. I'm so happy for him, he's put his heart and intellect into this book. I think it's revived him somehow; he's seems so…very…"

"Passionate?" offered Becky.

"As much as I hate that over-used adjective, I can't deny it. Yes, passion is the right word."

"Good, he needs passion. I think we sometimes take his equanimity for granted, he's a human being too, not only a priest, after all," observed Becky.

"I know, I can't imagine life without any passion," said Lidia, taking a gulp of wine.

"Me neither. Anyway, how's the tribe? Nick doing well?"

"Oh, he's fine, quite frisky, but not really following doctor's orders. He's increased his veg intake and cut back on the carbs, wine and red meat, but hasn't taken-up any other health regime; however, that's gonna' change come Christmas, 'cause I have a big surprise for Mr. Ponti," Lidia said resolutely.

"Don't tell me you've booked another health spa weekend up north. You know what a disappointment the last one was after his disastrous birthday,"

Becky said, while carefully twisting a long string of Emmenthal around a broccoli floret.

"Yeah, I know, he just hid-out, ordering room service, binge watching *The Sopranos*. But ironically, loved it! Said it was one of the most relaxing vacations he's ever had, his only complaint was that the food was so veggie-based he started to double-order...the room service bill was enormous. You know he managed to gain five pounds on kale chips, carob almond milk shakes, cauliflower pizzas and quinoa soy burgers!" They both laughed, Becky nearly choking on her broccoli.

"Anyway, the short answer to your question is; no. I'm never doing the spa thing with Nick again, although I could use it. No, I have a new strategy for Nick, requiring a much longer commitment, but one that'll be motivating," Lidia said smugly.

"So c'mon, tell me what this new 'motivating strategy' consists of," Becky urged.

"It's a surprise. You'll find out at New Years," Lidia replied, greedily dipping into the molten cheese with a chunk of tangy pumpernickel.

"Mmm, that is just too scrumptious; I could live on gooey cheese, bread and wine; although my waistline and liver may not like it...damn them. I don't know why, but lately I'm ravenous for luscious treats," Lidia flopped back on the cushy seat, absorbing the respite from an intense work week this delicious, cozy moment offered.

"That can't be mine." Lidia scowled, as the insistent ring of Becky's cell phone, interrupted her reverie.

"Sorry, Lid…forgot to turn the damn thing off. It's Danielle, mind if I get it?" Becky already had the phone to her ear, as Lidia consoled herself with another dip into the fondue pot.

"What? No Danielle, I've already booked our accommodations and flights. All the plans are made; I really can't change them now. Well, maybe you can take a long weekend together at Valentine's? Shouldn't be too difficult, seeing as your dad's your boss. Look, I have to go, I'm having dinner with Lidia. Okay, talk later…

Sheesh! Try and organize a nice family Christmas getaway and it seems all my youngest wants is to get away from her family," Becky sighed and took a deep drink of wine.

"Family getaway?" Lidia said, surprised, "you mean with you, Paul and the girls…all together?" she sat upright, eager to know more.

"That's right. We thought that since the girls were still single and unencumbered, we should take advantage of this time and at least spend one week at Christmas together, destination to be democratically decided. I voted for sun and sand, Paul and the girls for snow and skiing. So, we're off to a lovely ski resort in the Eastern Townships where I got some perks," Becky explained.

"Whoa! Does Paul really understand that this is just a family get together, and not a 'get back together'?" Lidia's voice rose with concern.

"We all have separate rooms, and yes, I made my intentions clear. The only worry I have about Paul is his knees, they're a mess, occupational hazard. I'm guessing he's just gonna down a lot of Advil and put on a brave face so as not to let his girls down. He wants to show them that their dad is no feeble codger. I just hope he doesn't break a leg in the process," laughed Becky.

"Or anything else," worried Lidia, beneath her breath. After swallowing a sip of wine, she inquired, "So, what's up with Danielle? Why doesn't she want to go?"

"It's not so much that she doesn't want to go with us, it's just that her new boyfriend booked an Airbnb villa in Puerto Vallarta with a bunch of friends and Danielle wants to join him for three days, then fly to Quebec to meet up with us for the remainder of the week, which is a no go! I know what she's up to, if I agree, she'll just send me a whiny text from Mexico saying she *really, really, really* needs to stay with Max at the villa for the rest of the vacation, and can't we just have fun without her?" Becky scoffed.

"Do you like this boy?" Lidia asked, her intuition hinting at the answer.

"No, not really. He's too cocky, in every way, if you know what I mean," Becky raised an eyebrow.

"Ah! The 'sex haze' phase, is it?" Lidia chuckled.

"Oh yeah, Danielle's got it bad," Becky sighed, pouring out the last of the wine in their glasses.

"Hysterical hormones…I'm so glad we're over that, although my husband seems to be in his second spring." Lidia scooped-up the last stringy bit of cheese from the bottom of the pot.

"Exactly, they can pop-up fiercely when you least expect it," Becky said laughing, draining her glass.

"Oh, speaking of cockiness and things popping-up unexpectedly, Javi's coming back to Toronto and wants to have Christmas dinner with us. Says he needs our help with a personal matter…I can't imagine what it could be. He's usually quite a closed book when it comes to the deep and personal, not like him to reach out," observed Lidia thoughtfully.

"Well, I just hope he hasn't got his nubile girlfriend 'up the duff'," cracked Becky with a smirk, "my god, can you imagine Javi a father?"

The mere thought of it made them laugh so hard, their ribs ached.

QUANTO BASTA

LIDIA SAT IN her living room across from Jesse and Athina, both bundled in their winter coats, luggage waiting in the front porch for Josh to come and drive them to the airport.

"Thanks for everything, Lidia," Athina said.

Lidia reached out for the girl's hand, "I'm just back-up," she smiled.

"Don't underestimate that. I was falling into the abyss. You, and Jess pulled me out."

"You're doing great now. You need to forgive yourself and live your life," Jesse said, still concerned for her friend's emotional state.

"I know, but I'm glad you're coming with me. I'm still really nervous about facing Ainsworth, making peace with him. When I have closure, I can properly start my life again, alone or not."

Lidia sat quietly contemplative, then looked at Athina, "There's one thing that I wish you'd consider, and that's telling your mother, I just know she would be devastated if she found out that you didn't turn to her too. I certainly know how I would feel if it were Jess."

Athina responded quietly, "I appreciate what you're saying, Lidia. But I really need time to be comfortable in myself again before I can tell mom. So, please let me do this in my own way, okay?"

"I won't betray your trust, I just want you to know you can trust your mother as well," Lidia said, smiling.

"Understood," Athina nodded.

Just then, a horn sounded from the curb, Nick came pounding down the stairs to carry the bags, give his two girls hugs and kisses, then taking Athina's hand he gave her an envelope and a little muslin sachet.

"Oh, what's this?" she asked.

"It's my recipe for tagliatelle alla Bolognese, you might want to make it when you mend things with Ainsworth," Nick suggested.

"And this? What's this for Nick?" Athina turned the little sachet over in her hands.

"That's some coriander, don't forget to add it to the sauce, to bring everything together... to make it sweet."

"How much do I use?" asked Athina.

"*Quanto basta...* when it's enough. Just trust yourself," Nick said meeting her gaze with a gentle smile; then stepping back, he joined his wife on the sidewalk, where they waved their goodbyes and hugged each other against the cold.

A SOFT LANDING

AN AUTHORITATIVE VOICE came over the intercom instructing Porter Airline passengers to put their seats and food trays in the upright position, fasten seatbelts in preparation for landing. Their ETA at Billy Bishop Airport was 1:30 p.m., and surprisingly for November, the weather conditions in Toronto were dry and mild.

Jesse pulled-out her ear buds, and obeying the disembodied voice, scraped-up the three remaining smoked almonds from the salty bottom of their cello pack, drained the dregs from her beer and assumed the upright, buckled-in position for landing.

She was elated, not only because Athina and Ainsworth made-up, but for Josh's proposal to her before she left. When he found that his tenant above the store, Black Jack, erected a solar-powered greenhouse grow-op on the flat roof, Josh served him a notice of eviction, a timely coincidence as he felt he and Jesse should take the next step in their relationship and move-in together.

She had wanted to think it over while away in Montreal, distance offering an objective perspective, but Josh was so excited at the prospect, that she relented and agreed before she left. Now she was really committed and finally felt 'all grown-up'.

Before she left, she and Josh had fun picking-out paint colors, writing-up a shop and scrounge list of furnishings and necessities, agreeing to abandon their summer Mini Cooper 'tour de France' plans, for now at least. And while she was away, Josh was busy sanding and staining the floors. They planned to finish the decorating together over the holidays.

But these were plans she deemed best to keep to herself until the New Year, a fitting time to ring in the changes. And while she guessed her mother would be anticipating her announcement, she worried that her nonno and dad would feel the empty nest most acutely, so instead of casting a shadow over their Christmas celebrations, she would wait, feeling fit to burst.

Pickles

NOT SINCE HIS daughter stopped believing in Santa Claus had Nick risen before eight a.m. on a Christmas morning. But this Christmas was different somehow; he felt a surge of excitement well-up within him. Bored with watching the clock as his wife snored away, and the rest of the house was quiet, he decided to go downstairs, plug-in the tree's lights, get the fire log going and brew some coffee.

While the coffee brewed and Nick hummed, whisking-up his waffle batter, to the tune of 'Jingle Bells', he was suddenly aware of being observed. Turning quickly to look behind him, he was confronted by his intruder, a very fluffy little white and brown canine, who upon making eye contact cocked an ear, vigorously wagged its tail, flicked its little pink tongue, anticipation shifting from eyebrow to eyebrow, if dogs can be said to have eyebrows.

"Well, and who might you be, my good man?" chuckled Nick, delightfully surprised, reaching behind the big red bow on the dog's collar to read the attached card: *Hello, my name is Pickles and I am your dog.* He petted the dog for a moment, then picked-up the warm little bundle, carrying it to the living room where his family had snuck-in, sitting silently in eager anticipation, dying to shout, "Buon Natale!"

"So, which one of you was brave enough to incur the wrath of Lidia, eh?" he smiled, standing in the doorway, rubbing his new companion behind the ears.

"Uh, well no one Nick, Pickles is a present from me," Lidia confessed.

"From you cara, and how's that? I thought you were adamant, 'No dog!'" the animal in question eagerly licking his face, wriggling in his embrace.

"Well, recently Clive and young Pickles moved-in with Shelton, Barney and Beelzebub, Shelton's two Siamese cats. Unfortunately, they just wouldn't accept poor little Pickles, bullied him until he had terrible anxiety, it got so bad Clive had to cage him before leaving the house.

They decided Pickles needed to have another address. So, I offered to take him as a Christmas present for you, since walking this beast will get you some exercise," Lidia said, smiling, as the new addition to the Ponti household broke free from Nick's embrace and made his inquisitive rounds of the family, enjoying the attention lavished upon him.

"Well, what more can I say except, thank-you cara, Pickles is the best present," he said giving his wife a loud kiss. "One question though, how did he come by his unusual name?"

"Oh that, Clive called him Pickles because he loves bread and butter pickles, is mad for them apparently," Lidia explained.

"Is that so, well I think I have a good recipe for them somewhere amongst my collection of Junior League cookbooks," Nick said, reaching for one from the shelf. Then sitting back in his wing chair, Pickles curled up in his lap, "Ah! Here it is, Pickles. I remember making these and look boy, I've even made a note in the margin, yes...*just needs a pinch more coriander*, you'd like that now, wouldn't you Pickles?"

Pickles leapt from Nick's lap and made a bee-line for the front door, barking insistently.

"Oh, maybe he needs to go out," Lidia motioned to Nick.

"No mom, it's someone in a town car," observed Jesse, standing to better see the street from the front window.

"Shouldn't be Javi, he's not due until six," Nick said starting out of his chair.

"Uh, looks like a tall girl with a mauve mullet, wearing very cool, Miz Mooz pirate boots...I'll go," Jesse scooped-up Pickles then opened the door to the girl, just as she was poised to ring the bell, "Can I help you?" she inquired of the startled figure.

"Um..." the girl looked back over her shoulder, as a man emerged from the car and bounded-up the front steps, both arms bearing gifts.

Jesse stared wide-eyed from the girl to Javi, then shouted down the hall, barely stifling a giggle, "*Daaad!* There's someone here to see you!"

A Christmas cracker

"Well, do we have to sing a carol or something before you let us in?" Javi asked a non-plussed Nick, standing wide-eyed at the door.

Recovering himself, Nick exclaimed, "Oh no, of course not, come in, come in!"

Upon hearing a familiar voice, Lidia rushed out to meet their guests and relieve Javi of his burden of shiny, beribboned parcels. Jesse helped Javi's young, leggy companion out of her bright blue leather jacket and into the living room, where she sat uncomfortably silent, surrounded by strangers.

Ignoring his companion, Javi followed Nick to the kitchen, where they engaged in a heated exchange.

"What the hell, Javi? I thought you weren't coming until six; I'm still in my pajamas! And who is that girl? Please tell me that's not 'the girlfriend'," Nick whispered emphatically.

"Relax, Nick. I had to come early; I had an emergency, fires to extinguish, so to speak. And no, Lucinda's not 'the girlfriend', that's over. She is in fact, my daughter." Javi exhaled deeply, plunked himself into a chair at the kitchen table and rested his head in his hands.

"Your daughter? Since when did you have a daughter?" Nick, indignant, stood over his friend.

"Since nineteen-ninety-seven, or so my birth certificate informs me," came the sarcastic response from the tall, mauve-haired girl in the doorway. "And don't think I'm any happier about it than my 'father' here." She pointed at the seated figure.

"Uh-huh," Nick stalled trying to take it all in. "Well Javi, care to introduce us?"

"Nick Ponti, meet my daughter, Lucinda Correia-Ortiz, late of Argentina, and the pricey, Toronto private school, Our Lady of the Seven Sorrows," he said, with a lax wave of his hand towards her, not deigning to look-up.

"Merry Christmas Lucinda, and welcome. It's a pleasure, to say nothing of a delightful surprise to meet you," Nick greeted her, extending his hand.

"A surprise? Yeah, I'll bet...you never even told them about me, dad!" Lucinda yelled, neglecting Nick's hand, she picked-up a whining Pickles. "This dog probably needs a shit." She stomped past the two men and out into the cold garden.

Nick took a seat across from his friend. "Well, she certainly has a good command of English," he remarked, bemused.

"Oh yes, better than you can imagine! She speaks the lingua franca like a stevedore," Javi laughed despite himself.

"She's not shy either, quite forthright in fact. Useful qualities for a girl in this day and age."

"Oh please, spare me. She's a nightmare. Her stepfather calls her Lucifer…not to her face, obviously. She'd kill him if she knew." Javi craned his neck to get a view of the garden but couldn't see his daughter. "Oh good, she's not there, probably went off to the park with that poor dog. Whose is it anyway?"

"Mine, but never mind that now. You and I need to talk." Nick nodded towards his wary friend.

"Alright, but first, do you have any grappa?"

Nick got his second-best bottle of grappa from the cupboard above the sink. He wasn't sure he wanted to squander his best on this occasion.

He put the bottle down in front of his friend, then started some espresso. "We're not going to drink this straight. We'll have a nice strong 'coretto' instead. We haven't even had our waffles yet. I expect Lucinda might want some breakfast too. So just hit the highlights, fill in the blanks later, ok?"

"Fine. The highlights…well, back in nineteen ninety-four, I was in Mendoza on business, met Valentina Correa, scion of an influential wine-making family and became engaged."

"Yes, yes, I remember. You were going to join the family business, marry this Valentina and settle down there in Argentina. You were there for about four years, weren't you? Then you turned-up here, wedding off, no drama, said there was nothing to report," Nick recalled, pouring their coffees.

"I was saving face. Valentina's family was hostile to me from the get-go, which is probably what made me attractive to her; she's a very rebellious woman. Although, she has to be, what with four over-bearing brothers and a mother who made Margaret Thatcher look like Mother Theresa," Javi said bitterly, stirring his coffee.

"Well then, I can see where Lucinda gets her, ah, 'assertiveness' from," Nick said diplomatically, pouring some more grappa into Javi's cup.

"Yep, a chip off that ol' block is my daughter, and a real 'Christmas cracker', full of surprises. You know Nick, I tried, I really did. But it became obvious the family didn't want me; they wanted money; I gave them money. Still, they wouldn't really let me in to the business or the family; I suspect they got immigration to complicate matters too.

"Valentina went cold, had all she wanted, a baby, directorship in the company…I became surplus to requirements. So, I walked away, left my shares to Lucinda, and that dream behind. And now I have the daughter back, as her mother and new husband Hans, are weary of her too." Javi shrugged, downing his coffee.

"You should've confided in me." Nick put a hand on his friend's arm.

"Why? I just wanted to forget about it, not be a figure of pity. I don't mean that I wanted to forget about Lucinda. She was such a cute baby," he said with a sigh. "Maybe though, for a time I needed to push that back too. Anyway, I did go back to Argentina, at least twice a year to see her, and when she was old enough, we corresponded and later, Skype. But really Nick, I felt more like an uncle than a father." Javi cast his eyes downward, contemplating his empty cup.

Nick felt a sudden urge to put an arm around his beleaguered friend but stopped short. "So, what can I do to help?"

"I was hoping you could wave your magic 'daddy wand' to help me cope with her, now that she's landed in my lap and in Toronto for the foreseeable." Javi let out a hollow laugh.

"I think that's going to take a lot more than magic. But we'll see what we can do. I'll help you all I can Javi, Lidia too, I'm sure." Nick poured him a shot of grappa. "In the meantime, I'll dress, you heat-up the waffle iron and we'll get everyone fed."

"Like to come out of the cold, to my place, after you finish your smoke?" Jesse said, startling Lucinda, who was shivering in the Ponti's mutual alleyway.

"Oh!" Lucinda quickly extinguished her smoke. "Uh sure, thanks, ah… Jesse?"

"Yes, that's right. Come down to my flat Lucinda, it isn't glamorous, but it's private and it's mine."

The girl followed Jesse to the garden entrance of her basement flat, Pickles, trailing eagerly behind.

Lucinda and Pickles settled into Jesse's couch, surrounded by big, colorful silk pillows. She looked with great interest at the large, unframed collages hung on all the walls, the whole room sparkled with the light of an elk horn chandelier, strewn with strings of fairy lights.

In the corners were brass planters, securing an array of tall bare branches, spray-painted in bronze, gold, and silver, set amongst them were accents of curly willow, painted electric blue. A huge glass bowl of mirrored stars sat on the brass Moroccan coffee tray, supported on the backs of two cinnabar ceramic elephants. "Wow, Jesse this is so cool! Who did the collages?" Lucinda asked in wide-eyed wonder.

"I did. Do you like them?" Jesse was pleased at

the effect they produced on her guest.

"Yeah, they're so intriguing; really deep…I feel I can look at them for ages and still discover something new…so many layers. Someday, I'd like to be an artist like you, or maybe first, a soccer star," Lucinda said earnestly.

"I'm still studying I'm afraid, but this coming year is graduation, finally!… So, you play soccer. What position?" Jesse turned the kettle on and set out two mugs.

"I'm a striker, a forward, was the best at St. Bart's. That's my old school in England, but at Our Lady's, there's no soccer…I hate boarding there," Lucinda confessed, lowering her eyes, chipping away at her silver nail polish.

"Oh, that's too bad." The kettle whistled and Jesse held up two paper packets, "So what's your pleasure Lucinda, hot chocolate or caramel mocha java?"

"Hot chocolate please. Do you have any cream?" Lucinda looked hopeful and hungry.

"Of course, you gotta have cream.," Jesse laughed as she prepared their drinks. She put a few Christmas cookies on a plate, then took it and the drinks to the coffee table.

Lucinda, ravenous, braved one scorching sip then reluctantly put her mug down to cool. Jesse offered her the cookies, she grabbed two, gobbling them quickly.

"Easy, girl! My dad's making us his Christmas breakfast special; Belgian waffles with strawberries, whipped cream and breakfast sausages with damson preserve. He'll be really disappointed if you can't clean your plate," Jesse warned.

Lucinda blushed, embarrassed, "Sorry Jesse, I didn't know. I haven't eaten since dad picked me up early this morning."

"That's ok. Don't feel bad," Jesse smiled at her guest. "Now tell me why you aren't 'bending it like Beckham' at St. Bart's anymore?" Jesse asked, sipping her coffee, interested to hear Lucinda's story.

"Apparently, they don't like 'recalcitrant students' or so the letter to my mother said. I don't see what the fuss was; my mom pays stupidly exorbitant fees for them to babysit me while she gets all lovey-dovey with Hans.

"All I want to do is study Art, Drama and play soccer. I hate the rest of the curriculum, I'm rubbish at Maths and Sciences, History and Geography are ok, but the projects are stupid. So why couldn't they just let me get on with what I like until graduation?"

"They expelled you, right?" Jesse arched an eyebrow.

"Yeah, anyway I didn't even want to go to boarding school. Hans convinced mom it would be good for me to improve my English, but they just wanted me out of the way. That's alright though, 'cause I hate them.

"While I was away, they sold my Appaloosa. Dad gave her to me, I called her Tango, she was so graceful. I loved that horse. When dad came to visit, we'd ride together. We got along then." Lucinda looked at Jesse, who suddenly realized just how upset and angry her young visitor was.

"I'm so sorry, Lucinda. I'll bet Tango was beautiful."

"Here, have a look at my beauty." Lucinda pulled her phone from her pocket and offered it to Jesse.

"Is that you jumping?" said Jesse, impressed.

"Yep, that's me and Tango at the Mendoza Pony Club meet. We came first in show-jumping that year," Lucinda smiled proudly.

After admiring the picture, Jesse, handing it back to her said, "It's so nice you and Javi get to spend Christmas together. After the break will you go back to boarding at Our Lady's or live with your dad?"

I don't know where I'll be living, but one thing's certain, I'm not welcome back at Our Lady of the Seven Sorrows," Lucinda said with a mischievous grin.

Oh? And why's that?" Jesse was wary of what the

answer might be.

Because my academic career there has literally gone up in flames," Lucinda started a fit of giggles, then caught her breath, "I was feeling homesick, for my abue, my late grandmother, and for the special choripan she used to make me. She called it super chori, it was sooo good, I can smell and taste it even now." Lucinda lay back against the cushions, closing her eyes.

"What's a choripan?" Jesse suspected it may have something to do with bread.

"Choripan is the best street food of Buenos Aires, it's a grilled chorizo sausage on a toasted bun topped with chimichurri sauce. But my abue used to cut the sausage and an onion in chunks, grill them together on a skewer, roll it all up with the chimichurri and some queso in a tortilla. It was so delicious and warm and melty with all the queso.

"So last week, I decided to treat my friends in the dorm to a little Christmas asado, a barbeque. I went to Walmart, got a George Forman Grill and all the other stuff I needed, one of the other girls got some Tequila and limes, it was gonna be an ace party."

"And the joke is…?" Jesse asked.

"The joke is that everything was sizzling along nicely, the skeleton staff were busy watching dvd's and boozing it up in the breakroom, when my skewers and all the grease caught fire. It wouldn't have been too bad if my wasted friend, Aisha, who is a hysterical ninny, didn't throw her tequila on the flames.

"The smoke alarms went off, then the sprinklers. And everyone was blaming ME! Blah, blah." Lucinda rolled her eyes and slumped back against the cushions.

"Well, I can see how they would hold you responsible, it was your party, after all," Jesse pointed out.

"I don't care. I'm only upset about George; he was well and truly toasted. Actually, it's a pretty good grill, if you don't set it on fire. You should get one, then we can have an asado party. I'll make you my abue's super chori, only this time I won't forget to soak the skewers." Lucinda's eyes lit up.

"Okay, but this time, we'll have to forget the tequila," Jesse said firmly.

"Oh," Lucinda said quietly, her enthusiasm, suddenly dampened.

Just then Jesse got a text, the girls' presence was required upstairs at the Christmas waffle breakfast.

AFTER EVERYONE'S APPETITE was satisfied, the

breakfast cleared away and the presents opened, Nick dozed by the fire behind a copy of the New York Times. Lidia, Jesse, Lucinda and Javi played three rounds of the board game, Word Thief, Javi's present to Lidia. The stake was losers do post-dinner clean up. Javi and Lidia won the rubber with 'antediluvian', which Lucinda insisted on looking up just to make sure she and Jesse weren't being hustled.

Father Frank appeared in time to help himself to some hefty eggnog and a plate of Aldo's Italian Christmas cookies, taking them to the den to join him in watching their favorite Christmas movie, It's a Wonderful Life. They never failed to get moony over the long-suffering Donna Reid and teary over the sappy ending.

Eventually, it was time for Nick and Javi to get cracking on the final touches to Christmas dinner. The piece-de-resistance this year was crown roast of lamb stuffed with wild rice, preceded by cream of porcini soup, then individual artichoke soufflés. The roast was accompanied by asparagus with Hollandaise and herbed new potatoes. The dessert was Jesse's favorite, flaming plum pudding with brandy hard sauce.

While Jesse and Lucinda lounged by the fire in the living room, sipping their mimosas and reading Lucinda's *People* magazine, speculating on whether bad boy, Justin Bieber, would dump his new girlfriend by next year. Then, could an Canadian-Argentinean wine heiress be in with a chance? If so, Lucinda decided her next hair color should definitely be an eye-catching ginger, although Jesse disagreed, figuring she'd have a much better chance as a blonde.

LIDIA WENT TO her room to freshen-up for dinner and share Javi's news bomb with Becky, who was enjoying some après ski time at the lodge.

"Get out! He didn't really just spring her on you this morning?" said an incredulous Becky.

"Absolutely, we couldn't believe it. We thought it was his lingerie model…she's quite tall, like her dad, and with the wild hair and not inconsiderable make-up, she could pass for about twenty, but she's only fifteen. Seems a bit wild, but quite sweet, once you get to know her. She and Jesse have really hit it off, thank god. Otherwise, I really don't know what we'd do with Lucinda, in any case it seems Javi actually doesn't. I think he's a little frightened of her."

"This, Lidia, I have to see; Javi intimidated by his teenage daughter. What's she doing in Toronto anyway? Don't tell me he has custody, what was her mother thinking? He couldn't raise a kitten, never mind a kid; he's too much of a kid himself." Becky winced at the thought.

"Oh yeah, he's got custody. It seems Lucinda's stepdad doesn't get along with her, so they packed her off to a British boarding school, where she failed everything miserably, except Arts and P.E. So, they packed her off again, this time to Toronto, to Our Lady of the Seven Sorrows, where her dad was keeping an eye on her. Sort of," Lidia smirked.

"What do you mean, 'sort of'?"

"Well, it appears that Javi's attention was diverted to his romantic involvement in Montreal instead, so Lucinda got up to some mischief involving a George Forman Grill, a pan of grease and some tequila. She nearly burned down her dorm."

"I guess she failed Home Ec. too then?" Becky roared with laughter.

"Oh yeah, and now Our Lady has one less sorrow than Javi, who is currently looking for alternate arrangements for the fruit of his loins."

"I think he's really going to need you and Nick. You'll help him, won't you? After all his mom's dead and the only sibling he's got left in Toronto, is sixty-two and childless."

"I know, I'll help to a point, but I think this is more Nick's section. I don't want to get too involved;

I'm done parenting. Especially teenage girls," Lidia said firmly.

"Okay, but you'll have to fill us in on the outcome at New Year's. Paul and I and the girls are coming if Danielle can tear herself away from Max... Yes, we're all having a good time, even Danielle, who nevertheless needs to sulk a little, if only for my benefit. Talk soon Lidia, and Merry Christmas!"

"And to you Becky, give the family our love." Lidia hung-up, then headed downstairs to organize the girls in setting the table.

LIDIA WAS PLEASANTLY surprised to find them already on task, so decided to join Javi and Nick in the kitchen, "Can I help?" she asked, peering into the soup pot.

"Sure, you can do the thyme. Here, I'll show you," Nick said, stripping the leaves off a sprig from top to bottom, then handed her a small bunch and the mezzaluna, with a wary smile.

As she worked away, Lidia noticed Javi was uncharacteristically subdued.

"So, Javi, have you decided what you'll do about Lucinda's school? If you want, I can get you some recommendations, with or without boarding, if that's your preference."

"Thanks, Lidia. But I'm not sure either way. I need to talk to Valentina, Lucinda's mother. Toronto doesn't seem to be working-out for Lucinda," Javi said quietly, head down, concentrating on trimming the lamb racks.

Lidia countered, "Don't you think you should talk to Lucinda first? It is her life, and she doesn't seem at all keen on her stepfather. You may just have to step-up to the plate here, consider her feelings. Provide her with a real home life, not just a school dorm and weekend outings," she looked-up at Javi, expectantly.

He sighed deeply, wiped his hands on his apron and stood back, hands on hips. "Look Lidia, I don't think living with me is the best option for her. I travel a lot, I'm not used to kids, never mind rebellious teenagers, I think either returning her to her mom, or leaving her in the care of professionals is the best course."

"You make her sound like a pet! She's your daughter, for god's sake!" Lidia was getting livid now.

"Hey, hey, that's enough Lidia," Nick said, banging his knife down on the chopping board, "Javi's just trying to do his best."

"Well, I just think, he can do better than dodging

this challenge, and making it seem the rational and responsible course, when it's not."

"Oh really?" Javi said with a smirk.

Lidia turned to face him. "Yes, really. And don't smirk at me. Lucinda is rebellious because she's been shoved from pillar to post, without any say. She's trying to get attention, your attention. So, give it to her, and not grudgingly.

"As for not being used to kids, just open your heart, follow the child, don't make her follow your dictum all the time. She'll cooperate if she's engaged in the decision-making too. Lucinda's a funny and sweet kid. Give yourselves a chance to be a family, Javi, you can do it," she said, putting her arm over his shoulder.

He stood beside her, thoughtful for a moment, then said, "You're right, Lidia. I haven't been fair to her, her mother either. And if her recent antics are an indication, Lucinda doesn't really want to live in a dorm.

"I'll ask her tonight what she wants to do, invite her to live with me, see how she feels about it. Then we'll find a school with a strong arts program, that's where she shines."

Nick, who was watching this interaction with quiet trepidation was relieved. "Bravo, Javi, and when you need to travel, she's welcome to stay with us, she'll be okay. She certainly hits it off with Jesse."

"Thanks, guys… guess I needed that shove, Lidia. If you ever want a job in sales let me know," he said laughing quietly.

AFTER A RICH, delicious dinner, replete with the pyrotechnics of brandy-soaked, flaming pudding, Javi and Lucinda left early. They needed to have a heart-to-heart at Javi's place. And whether it would become a place Lucinda could call home, only time would tell.

About the Author

Loretta Gatto-White is a former food columnist, freelance journalist, and anthologist. Her essays, and poetry have appeared in literary anthologies, journals, and magazines. Her stories have been translated into Italian, published online and in print. The books comprising, *A Pinch of Coriander trilogy* are her first novels.

Website: www.gattowhitewrites.com

Available now in paperback and eBook:

A Pinch of Coriander Trilogy
Book One: *Time Will tell*
Book Two: *The Truth About Secrets*
Book Three: *Long Way Home*